Praise for *Return to Life*

"These incredible cases are not simply solid grounds for accepting some form of reincarnation into our Western worldview. These are heart-rending, poignant reminders that many of us do not quite 'fit' into the cultural and religious worlds into which we are born. Obviously, we are more than these worlds. Way, way more."

—Jeffrey J. Kripal, author of *Authors of the Impossible:*
The Paranormal and the Sacred

"Researchers at the University of Virginia medical school's Division of Perceptual Studies are studying reports from children around the world who claim to remember their past lives. More than 2,500 such reports have been analyzed by the project's founder, Ian Stevenson, and several colleagues, among them Jim Tucker. Their work has immense implications for our understanding of the world and human nature, but has received relatively little attention from mainstream scientists and religious groups. *Return to Life,* like Dr. Tucker's previous book, *Life Before Life,* opens a door on this historic research. Even if you disagree with Tucker's brief speculations about the afterlife, you will get a good look at the kind of evidence for reincarnation that the University of Virginia team is assembling. It is astonishing to me that their work is not better known."

—Michael Murphy, cofounder and
chairman emeritus of the board of the Esalen Institute,
and coauthor of *God and the Evolving Universe*

"With *Return to Life,* Dr. Jim B. Tucker has driven a very large nail in the coffin of materialism. This is an important contribution to the growing body of evidence that consciousness survives the death of the brain and body. The fear of death and annihilation has caused more suffering in human history than all the physical diseases combined. This book is a powerful antidote to that dread."

—Larry Dossey, M.D., author of *One Mind: How Our Individual Mind Is Part of a Greater Consciousness and Why It Matters*

"*Return to Life* comes as a resounding wake-up call regarding human existence. For decades, materialists have insisted that consciousness is nothing more than a function or emergent property of the brain. But the fact is that scientifically, the origins and nature of consciousness and its role in nature remain a mystery. The greatest obstacle to illuminating these issues through scientific discovery is not ignorance, but the illusion that we already have the answers. The empirical evidence that Dr. Tucker presents in this book challenges the reductionistic, metaphysical beliefs of scientific materialism. If his research methods are flawed, the scientific community should bring this to his and the public's attention. If they are irreproachable, then the empirical facts he reveals compel us to reassess even our most fundamental assumptions about consciousness, human nature, and the universe at large."

—B. Alan Wallace, Ph.D., president of the Santa Barbara Institute for Consciousness Studies and author of *Dreaming Yourself Awake*

Return to *Life*

ALSO BY JIM B. TUCKER, M.D.

Life Before Life

Return to *Life*

Extraordinary Cases of Children
Who Remember Past Lives

JIM B. TUCKER, M.D.

 St. Martin's Griffin ✹ New York

www.stmartins.com

Designed by Omar Chapa

The Library of Congress has cataloged the hardcover edition as follows:

Tucker, Jim B.
   Return to life : extraordinary cases of children who remember past lives / Jim B.
Tucker, M.D. — First Edition.
     p. cm.
   Includes bibliographical references.
   ISBN 978-1-250-00584-7 (hardcover)
   ISBN 978-1-250-02086-4 (e-book)
   1. Reincarnation—Case studies. 2. Memory in children—Miscellanea—Case
studies. I. Title.
   BL515.T775 2013
   133.901'35—dc23

                                                            2013024015

ISBN 978-1-250-06348-9 (trade paperback)

St. Martin's Griffin books may be purchased for educational, business, or
promotional use. For information on bulk purchases, please contact the Macmillan Corporate and Premium Sales Department at 1-800-221-7945, extension 5442,
or write to specialmarkets@macmillan.com.

First St. Martin's Griffin Edition: January 2015

For Ian, in memoriam

Contents

1. A Comeback Kid? 1
2. Wandering Through Asia 18
3. The Boy from Barra 43
4. The Third James 63
5. He Came from Hollywood 88
6. Famous Names from the Past 120
7. Identity Unknown 138
8. Mind over Matter 165
9. Working on a Dream 195

Acknowledgments 221
Notes 223
References 233

It is not more surprising to be born twice than once; everything in nature is resurrection.

—VOLTAIRE

Chapter 1

A COMEBACK KID?

Patrick, a cute little boy with long dark hair and an impish smile, was my first case. He had just turned five when I met him and his family in their home, a compact house in a small Midwestern suburb. I was there accompanying Dr. Ian Stevenson. Once "a young man in a hurry," becoming the head of a psychiatry department in his late thirties, Ian had walked away from the ladder of academic success for an interest he would doggedly pursue for forty years—children who report memories of previous lives. Nearly eighty but with curiosity still unabated, Ian was meeting the family because Patrick's mother had become convinced her son was his deceased half brother returned to life.

Ian viewed Patrick's case as potentially important. Though he had published many articles and books about children who had made numerous statements that matched details of someone who had died, Ian's best cases were all from other countries, mostly in Asia, where a general belief in reincarnation existed. His American cases tended to be weaker. They included two basic types: children who seemed to remember being a deceased family member, and children who talked about a past life but did not give enough details for a previous person to be identified. The same-family cases had the inherent weakness that the child might have overheard others discussing the deceased. While Patrick's case was a same-family one, it had another critical feature: he had three birthmarks that appeared to match lesions on his deceased half brother, marks that had nothing to do with what he might have heard people say.

Ian arranged a three-day trip with a plan to be thorough. We would have a long interview with the family on the first day, a second one the next day to cover items we had overlooked or that we needed to clarify, and interviews on the second and third days with other people involved in Patrick's life. We hoped the extended time with Patrick would help him become comfortable enough to talk to us about any memories he had.

We arrived at the home and sat down in the living room with Patrick's mother, Lisa. Ian took a clipboard and a tape recorder out of his satchel, well-worn from his trips around the world. He tested the recorder and placed it on the coffee table. He began by asking Lisa about her deceased son, the one whose life Patrick seemed to be remembering. Ian asked, "That's not troublesome to you, is it, to talk about that?" Lisa said, "No. I mean it is, but no. Where do you want me to start?" Ian asked her to begin when her son first became ill, and with an even voice, she began the story.

Kevin had been born twenty years before. Lisa, a young mother, and Kevin, her first child, were doing well despite her split from his father, until Kevin began limping at sixteen months of age. This was intermittent at first, but after about three weeks he was limping all the time, and Lisa took him to his doctor. He was admitted to the hospital for three days and underwent various tests. A bone scan appeared to be normal, but x-rays showed extra fluid in his left hip joint. The doctor thought it might be infected.

Kevin was still limping when he was discharged. He fell two days later, and doctors at another hospital found he had a broken leg. They put his leg in a cast, but it caused the little boy so much pain they took it off after three days. At that point, he couldn't bear weight on the leg and refused to walk. Lisa took him to another doctor, an orthopedic surgeon. He ordered more x-rays, and these showed some destruction in two of the bones in his left leg. Kevin was again hospitalized. The doctor told Lisa he had a tumor in his leg. This difficult time was made even worse by the uncertainty of the situation. As Lisa said, they went through "probably a two-week period of being told he had leukemia, that he didn't have leukemia, it went back and forth." But the upcoming news would only be worse.

Kevin was transferred to a tertiary children's hospital to continue the workup. Along with his swollen leg, the doctors noted his left eye was bulging and bruised and he had a nodule above his right ear that might be a tumor. They suspected a neuroblastoma, a cancer that begins in nerve tissue somewhere in the body, often in the adrenal gland above one of the kidneys, and then spreads to other places. An x-ray of Kevin's kidneys showed a mass at the top of his left one. A skeletal survey found various lesions and an opaque area over his bulging left eye. On his fourth day in the hospital, Kevin was taken to the operating room. The doctors took a biopsy of the nodule above his right ear and inserted a central line, a large IV, in the right side of his neck.

The biopsy confirmed the diagnosis of metastatic neuroblastoma. At least a definite diagnosis had finally been made, but it was not a good one. Kevin began treatment, getting chemotherapy through the central line. The site where the chemotherapy entered his neck became inflamed at times, but overall, he tolerated the treatment well. He also started radiation therapy that would continue after he left the hospital, including to his left eye and his left leg. After ten days, he got to go home.

Kevin seemed okay for a while. Lisa showed us pictures of him. The first one was taken before he got sick, and he is laughing, a plump baby with lots of light, curly hair. The other two are from later. They reveal a thinner, bald little boy with bruising around his left eye, which looks displaced. Too young to understand he was dying, he appears happy in both pictures, beaming in one and exploring a toy fire station in the other. They are heartbreaking.

Kevin returned to the hospital six months after his first admission. He was bleeding from his gums because the cancer had infiltrated his bone marrow and it couldn't make enough platelets. He had also developed bruising around his right eye along with the faded bruising around his left. Lisa said he was blind in the left eye at that point. His disease was considered end stage by then, meaning the little boy would die soon, but along with a platelet transfusion, he did receive one day of chemotherapy and one day of radiation to his right eye socket. He was discharged and died two days later.

Lisa talked about all of this in a calm, unemotional manner. This may have been because Ian and I focused more on the facts than any emotions. Ian did comment that she must have been very affected by Kevin's death, but when she gave little response, we moved on to other matters. We were not expecting her to pour out her heart to us, and we were asking a lot just to have her recount the events of his illness and death.

Lisa carried on after Kevin died. Long separated from his father, she had started dating a new man before Kevin got sick. They married following Kevin's death, and Lisa soon gave birth to a daughter, Sarah. The couple divorced after four years, and Lisa later remarried again. She had a second son, Jason, and then, twelve years after Kevin died, gave birth to Patrick by C-section. She said that as soon as the nurses handed Patrick to her, she knew that he was connected to Kevin in some way. She didn't have that feeling when her other children were born, but this birth was different somehow. Lisa said she felt empty after Kevin died, wanting him back every day. When Patrick, her new son, was brought to her, she imagined a weight being lifted as her grief for Kevin was released. While Lisa saw a physical resemblance between the two boys, there was a link that went beyond that.

She soon noticed a white opacity covering Patrick's left eye. The doctors diagnosed it as a corneal leukoma. Patrick was seen by an ophthalmologist and examined periodically. The opacity shrunk after several weeks but did not completely disappear. While his vision was hard to assess with any precision when he was very young, he was essentially blind in his left eye just as Kevin had been blind in that eye at the end of his life.

Lisa also felt a lump on Patrick's head above his right ear at the same location where Kevin's tumor had been biopsied. When we examined Patrick, we felt the nodule above his ear. It had migrated slightly behind his ear by the time he was five, but Lisa said it was directly above the ear when he was born. It was hard, elevated, and more or less round. We measured it at about one centimeter in diameter. It was not tender at all, and Patrick let us press on it as much as we wanted.

Patrick was also born with an unusual mark on his neck. A dark slanted line that was about four millimeters long when we met him, it looked like a small cut. It was on the front of his neck on the right. This was the area where Kevin's central line had been inserted, though we had trouble confirming which side of his neck had been used for it. When we reviewed Kevin's medical records, we searched to find documentation of the central line's location. We finally found one mention in an operative note that was fortunately one of the more legible handwritten notes. It listed the procedures, including "Insertion of central line (Ext. Jugular), tip in SVC or Rt. Subcl." Translated into English, that meant the IV had been placed in the external jugular vein, which is a vein on each side of the front of the neck. As it was snaked in, the tip of the IV had ended up either in the right subclavian vein running below the collarbone, which the external jugular feeds into, or all the way to the superior vena cava, which carries the blood from those other veins into the heart. The keys for us were that it was the external jugular, meaning the IV was inserted into the neck, and that it was the right subclavian, meaning it was on the right side of his neck, where Patrick's birthmark was.

One of the most inexplicable features of the case was that Patrick limped once he got old enough to walk. He had an unusual gait in which he would swing out his left leg. This matched the way Kevin had walked, since he had to wear a brace after breaking his leg. We asked Patrick to walk across the room several times, and he was still limping slightly at age five, even though he seemed to have no medical reason to do so.

When Patrick was four years old, he began talking about Kevin's life. The first thing he said was that he wanted to go to the other house. Patrick talked about it for a while and seemed desperate at times to go there. Lisa asked him why he needed to return; was there a certain toy or clothes he wanted? He answered, "Don't you remember, I left you there." She answered,

"Yeah, but you have me here now." Lisa asked Patrick what their home looked like, and he said it was "chocolate and orange." Lisa and Kevin's home, actually an apartment rather than a house, was indeed a brown and orange building.

Patrick began talking about events from Kevin's life, coming out with statements at unpredictable times. If Lisa tried to get him to talk about Kevin, he usually wanted no part of it. Later he might mention him out of the blue. Lisa was getting ready for work one day when Patrick asked if she remembered when he had surgery. After she told him he had never had surgery, he said, "Sure I did, right here on my ear" and pointed to the spot above his right ear where Kevin's tumor was biopsied. Lisa asked him to describe the surgery, but he said he didn't remember it because he had been asleep.

Another time, Patrick became excited when he saw a picture of Kevin. He had never seen it before because Lisa didn't keep pictures of Kevin up in the house. His hands shaking, Patrick said, "Here is my picture. I've been looking for that." He was definite as he said, "That's me." He also talked once about the small, brown puppy that stayed with the family. Lisa and Kevin had indeed kept a dog like that, one belonging to Lisa's mother when she moved into an apartment complex that didn't allow pets.

The week before we visited, Patrick was sitting back on the couch and asked, "Do you remember when we went swimming?" Patrick had never actually been swimming but described a day when Kevin swam in the pool at his grandmother's apartment complex. He said his grandmother was there along with his sister's father. He recalled how they had dunked the man's head underwater and mimicked the sound he had made as he came up for air.

Lisa also told us that Patrick had talked with his brother

Jason about heaven. When we asked Jason, he told us about a couple of instances, with Patrick once saying he wanted to take the family to heaven, especially his mother. The next morning, we visited Lisa's sister. She also spoke about comments Patrick made about heaven. She described similarities between Kevin and Patrick, their tendencies to be soft-spoken, timid, even tremulous at times.

After that, what we hoped would be a great opportunity ended up falling flat. We took Patrick and Lisa to the apartment building where Lisa had lived with Kevin. Patrick had stopped talking about that home a while before, but we hoped that seeing it would spur his memory. We weren't able to go inside their actual apartment, and Patrick didn't show any signs of recognizing the building. He did say something about a race car track, which Lisa thought referred to one Kevin had there, but since he described playing with it with Jason, I didn't know what to make of it. We did at least confirm that the building was brown and orange.

We then met Patrick's father at his work. He said Patrick's lesions—the opacity over his eye, the nodule on his head, and the scar on his neck—were definitely present when Patrick was born. He said Patrick hadn't talked to him about Kevin's life, but he had overheard Patrick talking to Lisa about it. He thought the situation was bizarre but had accepted that Patrick was remembering Kevin's life.

We also met with Lisa's ex-husband, the father of Patrick's sister. He recalled all the time he and Lisa spent taking Kevin to and from medical centers. He didn't remember going swimming with Kevin as Patrick had described. Since that would have been at least seventeen years before, that wasn't surprising, though he did recall taking Kevin to the park one day. He had seen little of Patrick and was noncommittal about the possibility of previous lives, but he thought the situation with Patrick had helped ease Lisa's grief. He said Lisa had been extremely close to Kevin and suffered tremendously when he died. He told us he came to the interview because he hoped our study of the possible past-life memories might help her.

By the following day, Patrick became comfortable enough to talk with us. He often spoke softly, and that tendency, combined with poor enunciation, made him difficult to understand at times. Adding to the confusion, he sometimes talked about Kevin in the third person and about things they did together. I wondered if this was because Patrick, a five-year-old boy, had memories of Kevin's life but couldn't make sense of being another person.

He told us about going to the zoo with Kevin and their cousin. Patrick had been to a zoo once two years before but not with the cousin, while Kevin had gone a number of times. Patrick talked about Kevin's bedroom and its two closets. While Kevin's bedroom actually had only one closet, it had two sliding doors that opened on both ends. Patrick described an apple-shaped "water ball," and Lisa said Kevin had a bathtub toy like that. He also talked about going with Kevin to a ranch that had bulls. Patrick had never been to one, but Kevin had indeed visited a cattle ranch that his aunt owned.

Our trip was a success. We had learned all the history from Lisa, studied documentation of Kevin's lesions, and even gotten Patrick to describe some memories to us. Having enjoyed meeting Lisa and her family, I had a greater appreciation for the people involved in these situations. They were not just characters in the pages of Ian's reports. They were flesh and blood, and some had experienced the human tragedies that led to the end of a life a child later seemed to remember.

After we returned home, we wanted to calculate the likelihood that Patrick's defects matched Kevin's just by coincidence. Not even taking the limp into account, how likely was it
that a child would be born with three lesions that matched
ones on a sibling? Ian had previously determined that the
odds of two birthmarks matching wounds on another body by
chance were about 1 in 25,000. He began with the surface area
of the skin of the average adult male being 1.6 meters. He then
imagined that if this area were square and laid on a flat surface, it would be approximately 127 centimeters by 127 centimeters. Since he considered a correspondence between a birthmark
and a wound to be satisfactory if they were both within an
area of 10 square centimeters at the same location, he calcu-
lated how many 10 centimeter squares would fit into this body
surface area and found that 160 would. The probability that a
single birthmark would correspond to a wound was therefore
1/160. The probability that two birthmarks would correspond
to two wounds was $(1/160)^2$ or 1 in 25,600.

Critics challenged that figure. For Patrick's case, we decided to get some help. I met with two statisticians from the
medical school and explained the situation to them. Though
they seemed interested, one of them eventually sent me a report declining to estimate the likelihood. He said any calcula-
tions would oversimplify a complex system. He added, "Phrases
like 'highly improbable' and 'extremely rare' come to mind as
descriptive of the situation."

Ian had been intrigued by birthmark cases for a long time.
They drew on his interest in the interaction between mind and
body that dated back to his mainstream days in psychoso-
matic medicine. The year before we met Patrick, he published
Reincarnation and Biology, a two-thousand-page work, many
years in the making, that covered over two hundred cases of

children born with birthmarks or birth defects that matched wounds, usually fatal ones, on the body of a previous person.

While Ian was intrigued by these cases, I was initially uncomfortable with them. I didn't see how a wound on one body could show up as a birthmark on another, even if you accepted the idea of past-life connections. A student asked about this at a talk I gave. Ian responded with a quote from Charles Richet, a Nobel Prize–winning physiologist who also studied séances and ectoplasm: "I never said it was possible. I only said it was true."

That explanation did little for me. But Ian also wrote in *Reincarnation and Biology* about work that in various ways showed that mental images can produce specific effects on the body. An example was the case of a man who vividly recalled a traumatic event from nine years before in which his arms were tied behind him. During his recall, he developed what certainly looked like rope marks on his forearms. If images in a mind can produce specific effects like that on the body, and if the mind continues after death and inhabits a developing fetus, then I could see how the images could affect the fetus. It would not be the wounds on the previous body per se that produced the birthmark or birth defect, but rather the images of the wound in the individual's mind that did it. In Patrick's case, his marks seemed to match lesions that would have made a strong impression on Kevin: the blindness in his left eye, the scalp nodule that had been biopsied, and the IV site used for his chemotherapy.

Two years later, we visited Patrick and Lisa again. Patrick had continued to say unusual things. He had talked about a life prior to the one as Kevin, this one in Hawaii. He talked about his family there and a son who died. He mentioned a statue that melted due to a volcano and how the townspeople rebuilt it. From his descriptions, his parents believed he was recalling events from the 1940s.

Several months before we met this second time, Patrick began talking one night as his mother fixed dinner. He asked, "Do you know that you have a relative that no one talks about?" He said he had met this relative in heaven before being born. He was tall and thin with brown hair and brown eyes. He told Patrick that his name was Billy and he was called "Billy the Pirate." He had been killed by his stepfather, shot point-blank up in the mountains. He said he was upset that no one talked about him after his death.

Lisa knew nothing about any relative named Billy. When she called to ask her mother, she discovered that her mother's oldest sister had a son named Billy. The details Patrick gave were correct. Billy had been killed by his stepfather three years before Lisa was born. The murder was never talked about in the family. When Lisa asked about the nickname "Billy the Pirate," her mother laughed. His wildness had led to the nickname, and Lisa's mother said she hadn't heard it since Billy's death. There seemed to be no way that Patrick could have ever heard about Billy or his nickname before.

SCIENTIST WITH A VERY OPEN MIND

Patrick's story may sound familiar. I included a brief summary of it in my first book, and Carol Bowman, an author of two books on children's past-life memories who referred the case to us for Ian's unique type of investigation, wrote about it in one of hers. Ian had been hearing such stories for a long time. He was a singular figure. He could be the most prototypic, staid academician—formal at times and precise in his language—while exploring the strangest things. Exploring them did not automatically mean accepting them, and he never lost his analytic approach to every case he encountered. Patrick's mother said Ian reminded her of Jimmy Stewart, a comparison that, minus Stewart's folksiness, was pretty apt. Both were tall, lanky, distinguished older men with kindly smiles. Ian was also pleasant and supportive—unfailingly so as I took my first baby steps in the field—with a wry sense of humor he could on rare occasion use to devastating effect. His comment about a book whose author claimed was channeled from the spirit of William James, the great American psychologist and philosopher: "If the vapid writings . . . did indeed emanate from him, I can only say that this implies a terrible post-mortem reduction of personal capacities. (Survival of death with such an appalling decay of personality makes it, at least to me, a rather unattractive prospect.)"

Before focusing on this research, Ian had an accomplished academic career with dozens of publications to his credit when he arrived at the University of Virginia in 1957 to be chairman of the Department of Psychiatry. He also had longstanding interests in parapsychology and the question of whether any part of our minds survives after death. He started devoting more time to those interests and stepped down as chairman after ten years to focus on them full-time, mostly on children's reports of past-life memories. When he first began writing about the cases, journal editors knew him by his reputation from his mainstream successes. This led prominent publications to at least take note, offering respectful reviews of his various books. In a review of one of his books in 1975, *JAMA, The Journal of the American Medical Association*, said that "in regard to reincarnation he has painstakingly and unemotionally collected a detailed series of cases from India, cases in which the evidence is difficult to explain on any other grounds. . . .

He has placed on record a large amount of data that cannot be ignored." Two years later, *The Journal of Nervous and Mental Disease* devoted most of an entire issue to Ian's work.

He was far removed from those years by the time we met Patrick. Ian had always aimed for a scientific audience, writing densely detailed reports of cases for academic readers rather than the general public. The number of such readers open to considering his work had dwindled over the years, but Ian was still trying. At the end of our first trip to Patrick's family, we were eating dinner when Ian began discussing plans for a paper about Patrick's case. He imagined a title of "Unexpected Correspondence of 4 Physical Abnormalities between a Boy and his Deceased Brother," and he thought we should submit it to *The Lancet*, a British journal that is one of the leading medical journals in the world.

That proved to be too optimistic. Nine days after we sent the manuscript to the journal, we received a reply stating "after discussion among several editors here, we decided that it might be better placed elsewhere." We then sent it to another journal. And another, and another. In all, we submitted the paper to six mainstream journals over the course of a year, and none of them accepted it.

We eventually included Patrick's story in an article about several birthmark and birth defect cases that we published in the *Journal of Scientific Exploration*. It is produced by the Society for Scientific Exploration, an organization started by a group of academic scientists, including Ian, who had interests that the journals in their various fields were not friendly to, such as astronomers who studied UFO reports. The articles in it are thus scholarly efforts to address controversial topics. While our paper fit right in, Patrick's case did not reach the broader academic audience Ian had hoped for.

Nonetheless, his optimism was not entirely misplaced. The year after *The Lancet* rejected our paper, it published a letter from Ian about the forty-two cases of twins he and colleagues had studied in which at least one of the pair claimed to remember a previous life. The letter was more than a column long, and the journal gave it a title of "Past lives of twins" without even a question mark at the end.

When Ian died in 2007, the *Journal of Scientific Exploration* devoted an issue to reviews of his work and to people's remembrances of him. One was from Tom Shroder, an editor at *The Washington Post* who accompanied Ian on two research trips and then wrote a book about them. Shroder finished his piece by saying, "Whatever the truth turns out to be, Ian's work, those countless files filled to overflowing with the passionate precision of his research . . . well, they are something. They are really something."

The issue also included an article of Ian's from 1958 that may have portended his future. Called "Scientists with Half-closed Minds," it was an essay Ian wrote for *Harper's Magazine* that reviewed various examples of initial failure by the scientific community to recognize breakthrough insights. He warned of our tendency, especially dangerous in scientists, to reject new ideas that conflict with our previous understandings.

Ian's awareness of this pattern did not keep him from pursuing the work he thought was important. He once told me—with a smile—that he would die a failure because he had not achieved his primary goal of getting mainstream science as a whole to seriously consider reincarnation as a possibility. That objective may have been quixotic, but Ian expressed no regrets about the course he had chosen. To the contrary, he had enjoyed the journey, having been fortunate and resourceful enough to be able to devote many years of his life to studying matters that interested him. And though he may not have convinced the whole of mainstream science, he did open a lot of eyes, including those of numerous scientists.

Throughout his life, Ian kept the attitude of open-minded inquiry he encouraged in 1958. His final paper was a wonderful summary of his last forty years called "Half a Career with the Paranormal." He finished it by writing, "Let no one think that I know the answer. I am still seeking."

I hope you will approach the cases in this book with such an attitude. You may be tempted to think the idea of past-life memories is just too fantastic. I can understand that way of thinking. I'm not in this field because I'm a big believer in past lives, and I'm not here to promote the idea. I got involved in this work because I wanted to figure out for myself whether life after death might be possible. Even though I have become persuaded that something is indeed going on in some of the cases, I continue to consider the various possibilities for each one. I won't bore you with those considerations as I relate the cases, but I would encourage you to be open to all of them, both the ordinary and the extraordinary.

In my first book, I gave an overview of what is now fifty years of research. With this one, I'm focusing on some remarkable cases I've studied in recent years, ones I didn't include in the first book (except for Patrick's). But I want not only to show you the phenomenon but also to make sense of it. If you're having trouble taking this kind of work seriously, it may be because the cases can seem so outside of science, so outside of the real world. The *JAMA* book review notwithstanding, I suspect that's why many people have ignored this large amount of data for so long. At the end of the book, I'll address this concern, showing you how past-life memories can be consistent with current scientific understandings. If you are skeptical, I would challenge you to make a final determination only after you have heard all the facts. I will also explore how this phenomenon, beyond being consistent with scientific knowledge, can even lead to new insights about the true nature of reality, both about our existence in this world and about the possibility of life after death.

I hope all of us can try to emulate Ian's attitude of maintaining a critical eye but also an open mind. In this way, you can appreciate the astonishing experiences some of these families have had, and you can consider any meaning to take from stories of children like Patrick, a little boy who may have come to this life bearing marks and memories from his dear, deceased half brother.

Chapter 2

WANDERING THROUGH ASIA

While Ian wrote after decades of research that he was still seeking, my seeking was just beginning with Patrick's case. Nothing in the trajectory of most of my life had hinted that I would one day investigate reports of past-life memories. Growing up in North Carolina, I went with my family to a Southern Baptist church every week, and being the ever dutiful son, I believed what I heard on Sundays. I largely stopped attending church when I was in college at the University of North Carolina and stopped entirely when I left Chapel Hill and moved to Charlottesville to begin my psychiatry training at the University of Virginia. I left behind much of the dogma I had learned growing up. Though I did not reach a firm conclusion against spirituality, the leanings I had in that direction became quiescent.

I first heard about Ian during my training. I was intrigued that someone would do what he had done—walk away from a prestigious academic position to focus on a topic such as past lives—but not intrigued enough to contact him, and I never met him during my five years at the medical center.

After completing my training, I stayed in Charlottesville

and set up a private practice in a nearby community. I became interested again in spiritual matters when I remarried, as my wife, Chris, though not religious, was open to topics I had given little thought to, such as psychics, spirits, even past lives. I began reading a variety of books on such matters, including one by Ian Stevenson, *Children Who Remember Previous Lives*, that described his work with young children who reported past-life memories. Though I was not particularly drawn to the possibility of previous lives at the time, I was impressed that he had studied hundreds of cases over the years, using a careful, analytic approach I found appealing.

While I was reading the book, we saw in the local newspaper that his research division (then known as the Division of Personality Studies, or DOPS) had gotten a grant to study the effects that near-death experiences produce in the lives of the people who have them. In near-death experiences, people often report leaving their bodies and observing them from above, reviewing all the events of their lives, and going through a tunnel-like space to another world that may include deceased relatives and a bright light or a being of light. Since I was feeling unfulfilled with my private practice work, Chris suggested I call the division's office to see if the researchers needed any help interviewing patients for the study. When I called, I was invited to their next weekly research lunch.

As I prepared to attend the meeting, I wondered how people who did this kind of work dressed. For instance, did the men wear ties? I decided to go with the most casual work outfit I had, wearing a shirt and tie but not a dressy one. Ian then walked in wearing a three-piece suit.

I began going to DOPS every week for the meeting. After a while, I started working on a study to review the medical records of people who reported having near-death experiences, to assess how close they had actually been to death. It quickly became clear that we were also assessing the quality of the medical record documentation, as some of the records, particularly in the older cases, contained surprisingly few details. In any event, I enjoyed working with the others on the project, and even if it was only for a short amount of time each week, the project felt like a worthwhile, unpaid hobby.

After I had been coming to the division for almost two years, Ian asked if I would be interested in traveling to Thailand and Burma to study past-life cases with one of our colleagues, Jürgen Keil. I jumped at the chance and began making plans. Three weeks after our first trip to see Patrick, I set off to Asia for a month. In Bangkok, I met up with Jürgen, who had studied cases in Thailand before. German by birth, he had immigrated to Australia as a young man during the postwar years, originally as a fitter and turner for machinery. He then became a psychologist and held an emeritus position at the University of Tasmania by the time I met him. We connected with our translator and headed off to see cases.

CHASING AFTER A DEAD BODY

One of the first cases we saw involved a girl named Ampan. The case was old by the time we got to it—Ampan was nineteen years old at that point—but the details still seemed fresh in the minds of the people we talked to. Her parents said she started talking about a past life when she was five years old, older than many of the other children when they begin. She was crying one day and said she wanted to go home. Her mom said, "Your home is here. Where is the home that you're talking about?"

Ampan answered, "Buhom village." Buhom was three miles from the family's village. A paved road connected them when we were there, but witnesses said only a dirt road existed at the time, with buses rarely going between the two. Though Ampan's father had a distant relative in Buhom, her parents had never been there, and they didn't know of anyone from Buhom coming to their village to do business.

Ampan then told the story of a previous life. She said she had developed dengue fever and died at the district hospital. Dengue fever is a viral illness spread by mosquitoes in tropical and subtropical climates. It's usually not deadly, but a variant, dengue hemorrhagic fever, definitely can be.

Her parents asked Ampan what her name had been and she said "Wong" or "Somwong." They reported that she also gave a family name, but they didn't remember what it was. When her mother asked how she had come to them, Ampan said that after she died at the district hospital, a van took her body away. She ran after it but couldn't catch it. She then began walking, and after five miles she passed by the road in front of her parents' house. She said she was looking for drinking water. She saw her future mother, and there was a cool breeze. Rather than continue on her journey, she lay down to rest there, and she was subsequently born to her mother.

On that first day when Ampan told the story, she cried to go home. She continued to cry frequently, sometimes on a daily basis, for three years. Finally, when she was eight years old, thirty people from Ampan's village rented a bus to attend a merit-making festival, a Buddhist religious event, that was being held in Buhom. Ampan went with her mother and a family friend. When the bus reached Buhom, Ampan led her mother and their friend to a home where she ran to hug a woman there, calling her Mommy.

This woman had had a daughter named Somwong who had indeed died the way Ampan had described. We talked to

Somwong's parents, her sister, and her brothers. Ampan's mother had let them take Ampan in their home for some private time on that first visit. Ampan told them she wanted Somwong's Buddha amulet, a religious piece often worn as a pendant and thought to protect the owner from dangers. Somwong's family reported that Ampan told them where the amulet was and then found it. She also looked for some of Somwong's clothes, but they were no longer in the house.

After about an hour, Ampan's mother said they needed to leave, though Ampan didn't want to. She continued to visit after that, often two or three times a month, sometimes staying as long as ten days. Her parents, glad she was finally happy, did not object. They reported she still had the memories at age nineteen, which is much longer than these children usually report them, but we didn't get to meet her because she was away visiting friends. We tried again on a later trip, but she was away that time as well.

Though we didn't get a chance to talk to her, I was struck by her story. It offers interesting evidence for past-life memories, both in the way her statements corresponded to the other girl's life and with her apparent ability to find the girl's amulet. What impressed me most, however, was the image of a deceased spirit chasing after a van taking her body away from the hospital. She then tried to find her way back home after the van was gone. That longing to be with her family seemed to continue into another life, as Ampan cried so frequently to see them.

Her report of events between lives may seem surprisingly concrete; it's certainly not very ethereal. As I explained in my first book, only about twenty percent of these children talk about events between lives. For the ones that do, the reports can vary tremendously, some describing terrestrial events as

Ampan did, others saying they went to another realm like heaven. Some of this may be due to cultural influence, of course, but as I will argue later, there is good reason to think that the *afterlife*, if we want to use that term, is not homogenous. It can vary from individual to individual, there being not just one place (or two) where people go and not just one kind of experience that they have after they die.

In this case, if Ampan was indeed Somwong in a previous life, Somwong's consciousness (or soul or spirit if you like) seems to have remained tightly connected to this realm and to her family. This led to some anguish on her part during Ampan's early life but also to an eventual reunion. Somwong's attachment to her parents may have affected her experiences after she died and may have contributed to memories of that life carrying over to her life as Ampan. This would not mean necessarily that we will all have similar experiences after we die or that we all come back to live another life near our last one. I'll explore this further at the end of the book, but for now just consider that our attitudes in this life may affect what we experience after we die and perhaps even whether we come back here for another life at all.

ANOMALOUS DATES

Another case involved a boy named Juta, who was a little over four years old when we first met him. We visited his family in their home, a nice house in a small town in northeast Thailand where Juta lived with his mother and his grandparents. Four months after he was born, his maternal uncle, his mother's older brother, was killed in a motorcycle accident near Bangkok. He was hit by a truck, and his head struck the guardrail of a bridge.

Three or four months later, Juta developed respiratory

symptoms and a high fever for several days, his body shaking
and teeth chattering with chills. After he recovered, his family
noticed he had developed two dark spots on his left upper
arm, which were still clearly visible when we met him. They
were irregularly shaped, almost triangular, and about a quarter inch in diameter. They matched spots on his deceased uncle's left arm. His uncle had planned to get a tattoo there. The
procedure was so painful, however, that he stopped it after
receiving three spots as the start of the image, two of which
now seemed to be reproduced on Juta's arm. Juta also developed a protruding navel at that time, an "outie," as his uncle
had had.

Even though Juta's mother was his primary caretaker,
when he got old enough to talk, he called his grandparents
Mother and Father. His deceased uncle had been the only one
of their children to call them by the more formal expression
for Mother and Father, rather than Mom and Dad. And for his
own mother, whose name was Noey, he called her an expression that meant "Little Noey" or "Silly Noey." His uncle had
called his little sister this nickname to tease her, but no one else
used it. Juta's grandparents told us about this first, and when we
asked his mother about it later, she laughed and said she had to
threaten to spank Juta to get him to stop calling her that.

Juta showed other behaviors that reminded his family of his
uncle, especially when the uncle's friends came to visit. He joked
with them in the impolite way that buddies can do with each
other. He would put ice in several glasses, then pour beer or
whiskey into them and stir them with his finger, just as his uncle had done. He would distribute the drinks to his friends and
then drink one himself(!). One friend noted that he used the
same gesture pouring beer as his uncle had, pouring the beer
and then hitting the bottom of the bottle to get the last bit out.

When Juta was two, he said he had worked for a company in Bangkok building condominiums, which his uncle had done. He also showed a lot of interest in construction equipment. He would point to his uncle's motorcycle and say it was his.

We visited the family again eight months after our initial meeting. At that point, Juta was turning five, and he was no longer talking about his uncle's life. He had stopped calling his grandparents Mother and Father. Instead, he called his own mother "Mother" or "Mother Noey" (which was unusual). He no longer drank alcohol, refusing beer if given a glass, in contrast to his behavior at age two when he would drink a small amount of whiskey. The spots on his arm were becoming more faint. He seemed to be a typical little boy at that point.

This is an example of what Ian innocuously called an anomalous dates case. The dates were anomalous in that the child's date of birth was before the previous person died. The implication of a child developing memories of a person who died after the child had already been born is that a soul came into a young child and pushed out the soul that had been there before. Or perhaps the souls had an ongoing tug of war. Juta's family said his behavior had gone back and forth when he was younger, wanting alcohol on some days and not others. Perhaps two souls were battling for supremacy.

As odd as this may seem, it receives support from two of the most remarkable and perplexing cases that Ian ever studied. He investigated them with Satwant Pasricha, a clinical psychologist in India who, until her recent retirement, was a Professor of Clinical Psychology at NIMHANS, the National Institute of Mental Health and Neurosciences. The subject of the first case was a woman named Uttara, who at the age of thirty-two suddenly displayed a new personality. Uttara had been hospitalized due to several health issues when a yogi came to the hospital and gave instructions on meditation, including breathing exercises that induced a somewhat altered state of consciousness. Though Uttara had meditated in the past without incident, her behavior changed drastically this time, as she alternated between times of excitement and periods of silence. She would wander away from the hospital. Oddest of all, she began speaking in another language that her doctor thought was Bengali, the language from the Bengal area of India, which Uttara did not know. The doctor said his hospital could not take care of a patient behaving so strangely, and he instructed Uttara's parents to take her home.

This meant that they had to manage their daughter, who not only was acting very strangely but was no longer able to converse with them. She spoke a language they didn't know, and she could no longer understand Marathi, their native language. They initially had to communicate with her using gestures. They found Bengali-speaking people to talk with her and eventually picked up some Bengali words themselves. She said her name was Sharada. She gave many details of what she said was her life in Bengal. Though she apparently thought that life was ongoing, she seemed to come from another time, as she appeared completely unfamiliar with any tools, appliances, or vehicles developed after the industrial revolution. She did not recognize Uttara's family or friends. Sharada stayed "in control" for several weeks before Uttara returned to her normal personality. But her family was not done with Sharada. She continued to emerge intermittently for years. Ian and Satwant found out that Sharada appeared twenty-three times during the first three years. Most of the Sharada phases only lasted a day or two, but some were much longer, including one that went on for seven weeks.

In addition to discussing various locations in Bengal, including five obscure villages, Sharada gave the names of a number of people she said were her family members. The names were traced to a family that lived in West Bengal in the early nineteenth century. The names and relationships she gave for her father and six other male members of the family all matched a male genealogy of a family that was discovered. This genealogy had been published sixty-five years before in a Bengali magazine with a local circulation, but as Uttara had never visited that state, Ian and Satwant were confident she had never seen it. Since it only included the names of the men, they did not find conclusive proof that Sharada had existed as a real person, but her statements about her family were confirmed. It appeared that Uttara's body had been taken over by this personality named Sharada, a woman who had lived in another part of the country 150 years before.

Regarding Sharada's ability to speak Bengali, Uttara and her family said she had never learned it, other than taking a few high school lessons in reading Bengali script from a teacher who himself could not speak the language. One of the researchers' associates, Professor Pal, had four long talks with Sharada in Bengali, and he and five other native Bengali speakers all agreed that despite some imperfections in her speech, she had a solid command of the language. Ian and Satwant published a paper on the case, and four years later, Ian also wrote it up for a book. In the latter report, he noted that Uttara had been accused of having learned to speak Bengali in school, though the evidence for that was meager. He had also asked a linguist to listen to two recordings made of Sharada speaking and singing. The linguist said that based on the recordings, he did not hear indications of archaic speech that others had heard in conversation with her. He also said her accent was not native Bengali.

I'm willing to overlook the imperfections in her speech and accent. It's like Samuel Johnson's line about a dog walking on its hind legs: "It is not done well; but you are surprised to find it done at all." If the woman actually started speaking a language she did not know, that calls for an explanation.

Was this a case of possession by a Bengali spirit using the imperfect instrument of a woman who had never spoken Bengali? Or was it a bizarre case of dissociation, in which a woman, like patients with multiple personality disorder (now called dissociative identity disorder), suddenly took on the identification and behaviors of a different person? In this situation, however, she somehow displayed knowledge she seemingly could not have acquired in this life.

Ian corresponded sporadically with Uttara for thirty years after her adventures with Sharada began. Sharada was still coming even at the end, but only once a year for a brief appearance, and she did not affect Uttara's life at that point.

The second case involved a young woman named Sumitra. Ian and Satwant studied this one along with another psychiatrist, Nicholas McClean-Rice. Sumitra began experiencing episodes, lasting from a few minutes to an entire day, in which she would appear to go into a trance with her eyes rolled upward and her teeth clenched. During a couple of these, she seemed to be taken over by different personalities, one who said she had ended her life by drowning herself in a well and another who said he had been a man in another part of India. These culminated in a time when she lost consciousness and then, by all appearances, died. She stopped breathing and had no pulse for at least five minutes.

As Sumitra's family began grieving around her, she somehow revived. She initially appeared confused and said little for the next day. After that, she didn't recognize the family and friends around her. She said her name was Shiva and that she had been murdered by her in-laws in a place called Dibiyapur, some sixty miles away. She gave many details that were found to correspond to the life of one Shiva Divedi, who was unknown to Sumitra's family and who had died violently in Dibiyapur two months before Sumitra's transformation. On the day of her death, Shiva had been quarreling with her in-laws and told her uncle that her mother-in-law and one of her sisters-in-law had beaten her. The next morning, her body was found on the train tracks. Her in-laws said she had killed herself by jumping in front of a train, but when her uncle saw her body, he thought it was suspicious that her head appeared to be the only part of her that was injured. He asked Shiva's in-laws to hold off cremating her for four hours until he could bring her father there. They ignored his request, and Shiva's body was ashes by the time her father arrived. When Sumitra was later shown a picture of Rama Kanti, Shiva's sister-in-law, she said, "This is Rama Kanti, who hit me with a brick."

Sumitra, still calling herself Shiva, rejected her husband (and his amorous advances) and her son for some time and asked to be taken to Shiva's two children. Her family initially thought she had gone crazy and later that she had become possessed. They made no efforts to verify what she was saying. Eventually, Shiva's father heard a rumor that his daughter had taken possession of a young woman in a distant village. Three months after Sumitra's revival, he visited her. Sumitra recognized him and said she was his daughter. She ultimately recognized twenty-three people from Shiva's life, either in person or in photographs.

Sumitra's transformation also included changes in her behavior, as the researchers put it, "from that of a simple village girl to that of a moderately well-educated woman of higher caste and more urban manners, who could now read and write Hindi fluently." She wrote letters to Shiva's father, demonstrating writing ability somewhere between Sumitra's previously limited abilities and Shiva's educated ones. A letter found during a follow-up investigation (by Antonia Mills and Kuldip Dhiman) included lines like, "Papa I do not like it here . . . God is bad as he has dumped me here." A year after her revival, Sumitra once seemed to resume her original personality for a few hours. Otherwise, she had remained Shiva constantly for two years when the initial investigation was completed. Indeed, as the follow-up study determined, she remained Shiva all the way until the time of her death, thirteen years after her revival. Everyone, including Sumitra, seemed to gradually adjust to the new reality after her transformation. She warmed up to her family and presumably her husband, as she had two more children. Shiva's family stopped visiting after a while and let Sumitra live her life.

Satwant began investigating the case a month after Sumitra first met Shiva's father. She and Ian ultimately interviewed twenty-four members of the two families, along with twenty-nine other individuals for background information. Unless the case is an elaborate fraud perpetrated by a large number of people for no apparent purpose, the researchers seem to have documented a case of possession. In discussing this possibility, they wrote: "Although we do not dogmatically assert that this is the correct interpretation of this case, we believe much of the evidence makes it the most plausible one."

These cases are unusual, even by our standards. I present them to point out that while we normally think there is a one-to-one correspondence between a brain and a mind, that may not always be true. A basic assumption of modern neuroscience is that the brain creates the mind or consciousness we experience. So how could a consciousness, originally associated with a brain that is long since dead, take over the body of a living person? An alternative is that consciousness goes through the brain but exists outside of it. It would be a separate entity from the brain, normally linked to it quite closely for the duration of a life, but separate nonetheless. These cases in which a brain seems to have contained two consciousnesses that developed independently are much more consistent with this alternative theory than with the modern idea that the mind is what the brain does, end of story.

The normal course is for a brain to house only one mind during a lifetime, to be sure. But the rarity of these cases doesn't lessen their potential importance. As William James said, "If you wish to upset the law that all crows are black, you mustn't seek to show that no crows are; it is enough if you prove one single crow to be white." Cases in which the consciousness of a deceased individual appears to take over the body of a living person challenge the belief that a consciousness or mind is confined to one brain, which is wholly responsible for creating it.

AN UNFORTUNATE HUNTING ACCIDENT

Another case Jürgen and I studied in Thailand had some interesting twists to it. The child and the previous person lived in the same village and were in fact related, the child's grandfather being the older brother of the previous person's mother. The previous person was a young man named Boon who went hunting one day with three friends. One of them accidentally dropped his gun. It discharged, shooting Boon in the chest. The friend apparently panicked and ran off, but one of the other young men, a fellow named Phon, carried Boon's body out of the forest back to the village. Villagers tried to help, but Boon was dead at that point.

We talked with the man who dressed the body after the death. He reported that Boon had a wound on his chest under his left nipple that had bled profusely. The bullet had not passed all the way through the body, and Boon had a bulge on his back where the bullet was thought to be. It was a large area, blue with bruising, on the right side of his back below his shoulder blade.

Two months later, a boy named Somsak was born. His family reported he was born with a birthmark on his left chest and one on his back. Somsak was nine years old when we met him, and at that point, though the marks were hard to see and even harder to photograph, the one on his chest was still visible. Boon's mother, who saw her son's body after he died, told us Somsak's birthmark was in the same place where Boon had been shot.

Somsak's mother died of cancer when he was five, so we interviewed his grandmother and his aunt to learn about his previous behavior. They said that when he was first old enough to talk, Somsak woke up early one morning and asked his mother why Phon had shot him. He continued to ask this for the next couple of years. By all accounts, he was confused in thinking that Phon had killed Boon, since it was actually another friend's gun that had discharged, but he was upset at Phon anyway.

At the age of two, he approached Phon and said, "You are a murderer. You are the person who killed me." We talked with Phon, who said Somsak was so mad he tried to strangle him. After talking with us a bit, Phon said he didn't remember the events surrounding Boon's death and abruptly walked away. That death must have been quite painful to him, but I wondered if being called a killer, even if by a toddler, contributed to his discomfort.

We talked with Boon's parents, who told us that when Somsak was little, he was able to point out Boon's room in the house, and he correctly identified the pillow that belonged to each family member. He remembered items that had been Boon's, such as a saw and a locket. He took things that belonged to Boon but nothing that did not. Boon's parents felt Somsak still remembered them from his life as their son, calling them by the familiar names that Boon had. He was said to have recognized Boon's girlfriend as well, but she was away working in the fields and wasn't available to talk to us.

Somsak had also named four people who he said had walked past Boon's body after Phon brought it back from the woods. He refused to visit one of them when he was in the hospital because he said the man had ignored him back then. We talked with another one he named. The man explained his actions on the day Boon was shot. He had initially started out to help, he said, but he needed to go to a field to chase one of his cows that was in trouble due to flooding during the rainy season. When he saw Boon's parents behind him, he assumed they would take care of Boon, so he went to attend to the cow. He said he came back afterward, but it was too late to help at that point.

The man said no one else had ever said anything to him about ignoring the body. Yet somehow Somsak had known about it. As the man was rationalizing his behavior to us, I was struck by his need to explain himself because of a young boy's accusation about events from a previous life.

The following day, we spoke with Somsak himself. Even though he was nine years old by then and had stopped talking about Boon long before, we still wanted to see what he might say to us. He gave numerous details regarding Boon's death, some of which were incorrect as far as we could tell, but then acknowledged that though he still remembered being shot, he was mixing in details he had heard from others with his own memories.

I actually found this more credible than if, after several years of not talking about Boon, he would claim to still have perfect memory of his death. In general, we don't put much stock into what the child says years after the previous person has been identified. By that time, he or she may well have had an opportunity to hear all kinds of things about that person. What we focus on are the things the child says when the case first starts. Those are most impressive—when the child begins to talk about the life of a complete stranger. Here, even though Somsak was describing someone known to his family, the statements he made and the behaviors he showed made the case intriguing.

After Thailand, we headed to Burma. The country's name was changed to Myanmar in 1989 by the military regime running the country. That change has received varying degrees of acceptance, and most of its citizens seem to prefer the name Burma. The contrast with Thailand was striking. Thailand showed many signs of development, particularly in Bangkok. In fact, it was a scene of massive construction during my first trip there, as giant expressways were being built above its clogged roads, so that in some areas Bangkok looked like a futuristic city gone horribly wrong.

There was nothing futuristic about Yangon (or Rangoon), the largest city of Burma. The buildings were run-down, and modern skyscraper office buildings were absent. The people were very pleasant, however, and we saw cases in Yangon before traveling north to places such as Meiktila and Mandalay.

DISTINCTIVE MARKINGS

One of the cases we saw in Burma was an example of what Ian called experimental birthmarks, a practice I discussed in my first book. People in certain areas of Southeast Asia sometimes make a mark on a body after someone dies, with the hope that the deceased individual will take the mark to the next life. In that way, when a baby is born with a birthmark that matches it, people can identify the infant as the previous person come back. Ian studied twenty such cases, and Jürgen and I found eighteen more.

Yin Yin was a little girl who was seven years old when we met her. Her maternal grandmother had died of kidney disease nine years before Yin Yin was born. An hour or two after she died, her daughter (Yin Yin's aunt) used soot to make two marks on her body. One was on the outside part of her left leg just above her ankle, and the other was on the inside part of her right leg on and below her ankle. Several people saw her make the marks, including a neighbor we talked to. Yin Yin's mother did not see the marks but knew her sister had made them.

Before Yin Yin's mother became pregnant with her, she had three dreams in which Yin Yin's grandmother said she wanted to come live with her. In the dreams, Yin Yin's mother initially said no, but her grandmother became more insistent with each successive dream until her mother relented, telling her, "As you wish." A month later, she became pregnant. During the pregnancy, she had cravings for tea and cake, Indian spiced food, and milk. While she didn't normally like these, Yin Yin's grandmother, whose father was Indian, did.

When Yin Yin was born, she had birthmarks that matched both of the marks her aunt had made on her grandmother's body. We confirmed this with her family and with the neighbor. She had no other birthmarks, and her two brothers didn't have any either. Her two had faded away by the time she was six years old, so they weren't present for us to see a year later.

Yin Yin began talking at around eighteen months of age, and she made a number of statements related to the life of her grandmother. She asked about a mortar that the grandmother had owned, and when her uncle hurt his knee, she said that medicine should be pounded in the mortar and put on his knee. The grandmother also had a shell that she had used during ceremonies. Others in the family did not use shells, but during a ceremony Yin Yin asked about hers. Both of these questions came before she turned two, and as a youngster, she began talking about the previous life frequently. For example, she asked about her money and jewelry. Her grandmother had apparently been quite well off. The family developed financial problems after her death, and Yin Yin once asked why the family had spent her money. When she was being spanked, she would ask, "Why do you not respect your mother?"

The neighbor we talked to was known to Yin Yin's family as "Ma Win Kyi." Yin Yin's grandmother, however, had called her "Daw Win Kyi," and so did Yin Yin, even though no one around her did. She also called her parents and her aunt and uncle by their given names.

During World War II, Yin Yin's grandmother had lived with a cousin in Tavoy, a city in a different part of Burma. She called the cousin "Baby" and was the only person to do so. That cousin later lived with Yin Yin's family for a while, beginning when Yin Yin was five years old. Yin Yin also called her "Baby" and once said to her, "Please shut your ears because the English bombers will drop the bombs." Her family interpreted this as a reference to the bombing of Japanese soldiers in Burma by the English during World War II.

Feeling sad when they heard Yin Yin talk about the life of her grandmother, her family tried to discourage her from saying such things. They fed her eggs for a while in the belief, common in Burma, that this would make her forget about her previous life. That didn't seem to work, but her statements did become less frequent as she got older. By the time we met her, she generally talked about her grandmother's life only when she was angry or sad. Two days before we met her, however, she did say to her female first cousin, who was visiting, "You look like my son." The family said the cousin does, in fact, closely resemble the grandmother's son (the cousin's father), but he wasn't with her on the visit.

Along with her statements, Yin Yin had a habit that reminded her family of her grandmother: she would eat with one leg hiked up in her chair. She and her grandmother were the only two in the family to do that. This is similar to the behavior of a child Ian studied, a boy in Sri Lanka named Sujith. When he drank, he drew his legs up, just as the man whose life he seemed to remember had.

We talked to Yin Yin, but she didn't say much to us. She did report a memory of a group photograph being taken. Her family produced a photo that included her grandmother. Yin Yin didn't identify anyone in the shot, but she then said she remembered another photograph that had been taken in a particular room of the house, which she pointed to. Her family reported that a group photograph that included Yin Yin's grandmother had, in fact, been taken in that room twenty-five years before. The photograph had been given to other family members in Tavoy more than twenty years before, and Yin

Yin's immediate family members hadn't thought of it for many years.

ANIMAL BEHAVIOR

For the sake of completeness, I will mention that Yin Yin's aunt, the one who marked her grandmother's body, told us that she had also marked a dog one time. A boy was subsequently born in that family with birthmarks on his leg that matched the ones she had made on the dog.

This brings up the uncomfortable topic of past lives as animals. Ian wrote that he had to overcome his initial prejudice against such cases. (In fact, he once wrote in a letter that when he first went to Asia, he was inclined to ridicule such claims.) Once he managed to overcome that prejudice, he kept records on any claims about animal past lives and found them to be extremely rare. He pointed out that if cases were created purely by religious beliefs, we should expect to find more in South Asia than we do, since Hindus and Buddhists there believe that animals can reincarnate as humans and vice versa.

Most of the claims of past lives as animals are of course unverifiable. One strange case in Thailand seems to be an exception. Ian was traveling there with an associate named Francis Story when someone gave them a booklet about the case of a boy who claimed to have been a python in a previous life. Story wanted to study it, but as it was on the other side of the country, Ian thought it would be a waste of time and money. Nonetheless, after Ian left, Story did go to the site of the case and thought it seemed quite authentic. He talked with the boy, his parents, and his older sister. He was unable to talk to a key figure in the case, a Mr. Hiew, because the way to his village was under water and impassable, but Hiew had been interviewed for an article in a newspaper, the *Bangkok Times*.

The boy, named Dalawong, claimed he had been a deer in a past life. He said that after he was killed by a hunter, he was reborn as a snake. Just before Dalawong was conceived, his father had eaten snake meat when it was served to him by an acquaintance who had killed a python after an extended struggle. When Dalawong was three, that acquaintance, Mr. Hiew, came to a party at the house next to Dalawong's family. Neither Dalawong nor his mother had met him before. When Dalawong saw him, he became infuriated and tried to find a hammer or stick to use to attack him. He said Mr. Hiew had killed him when he was a snake and gave details of how the killing occurred. These were ones that Dalawong seemingly had no way of knowing, involving a particular cave and a fight between a snake and two dogs, followed by a confrontation with the owner of the dogs, who killed the snake. Hiew confirmed that all the details were correct. Dalawong said that after he was killed, his spirit saw his future father and thought he was kinder than the other men who ate the snake meat. He followed him home and soon entered his mother's body.

His father reported that when Dalawong met Hiew, he touched him on his left shoulder and said he had been bitten by a snake there. His father said that Hiew did indeed have a scar at that spot from a snake bite. The others didn't mention that aspect of the story. Dalawong got over his initial anger toward Hiew and said it was better to be a human than a snake. In fact, he began killing snakes as he got older, doing this out of pity because he said being a snake is very difficult.

Jürgen Keil visited Dalawong some twenty years after Francis Story met him. Dalawong still believed he had been a snake in his last life. He continued to visit the cave where the snake had been killed. He would go there every couple of months and meditate. During his meditation, he obtained information about using herbs to help the sick, and he was recognized in his village at that point as a local doctor.

I should also add that Dalawong was born with ichthyosis, a skin condition that caused his body, particularly the lower half, to be covered in scales. You might say they made his skin appear snakelike.

I may be well past your boggle threshold now, the point at which a story becomes too mind-boggling to accept. I confess this case approaches my own boggle threshold. But it is not entirely unique. I recently received an e-mail from an American mother writing about her son, Peter. One day when he was six, she gave him a candy necklace. He told her, "When I was a chimpanzee a boy threw one in my cage. I didn't know what to do with it." She asked him how he got in the cage, and he described falling into a trap and being taken to a zoo. She also asked what happened after he died as a chimp but before he got into "Mommy's stomach," but he only answered, "Nothing." Her husband then came home with their other children, and things got busy. When she later tried to ask Peter more about what he had said, he didn't even remember their conversation. If the candy necklace stirred a memory, nothing else ever did, because Peter never talked about being a chimp again.

I bring up the animal cases to make a point. Though I might be able to believe that a chimpanzee could have some conscious memory of a candy necklace, I certainly don't believe a snake would remember details about a particular location and a series of events, and years later be able to recognize a man who was its final nemesis. It's true I don't know what goes on in the mind of a snake, but that does cross my boggle threshold. What I can consider, however, is that a consciousness was associated with the snake while also being apart from it. Though the brain's activities would supply information to it, the consciousness would involve more than what was being recorded in the brain. It would transcend the physical. And this transcendental, nonphysical aspect could continue on after the death of the brain and the body.

This concept receives some support from cases of near-death experiences in which an individual's brain is not functioning. People often report memories of events that happened around them, ones whose specifics are sometimes later verified to be extremely accurate. The consciousness that was associated with the dying body is taking in new information (through some mechanism outside the five normal senses) even though the brain is not working. Many people in that situation report then leaving the physical and having out-of-this-world experiences.

This consciousness that these near-death cases suggest, which functions when the brain is no longer working, may function separately from the brain during life as well. Dalawong seemed to have an awareness of events in the snake's life in a way that the snake would not have had. This awareness belonged to the consciousness that he said continued on in spirit form after the snake died, before becoming attached to his present life.

All in all, Asia proved to be fertile ground for finding new cases. This was not surprising. The places I visited were ones where most people believe in reincarnation or are at least quite open to it. Word gets around when a child claims memories of a previous life. If the claims are compelling enough, reports of the cases may appear in newspapers. If our associates in those places are looking for cases for us to study, people can usually point them in the right direction.

The situation tends to be quite different here in the West. Many of the American families who contact us have told no one else about their children's statements. The grandparents and extended family may not know and may not be receptive to hearing about them. Cases only get into the media very rarely, and while I will describe one of those later, we are usually dependent on parents to send us their stories, as we have no other way of discovering them.

After three trips to Asia, I decided to focus on Western cases anyway. I enjoyed my travels with Jürgen, and we saw a lot of interesting cases. But it seemed to me that just collecting more Asian ones wouldn't accomplish a great deal; if Ian's two thousand Asian cases hadn't convinced people to take a look at the research, studying more was unlikely to do so. I hoped that Western examples might get people's attention in a way that the Asian ones had not. Though they are harder to find, some of them have proved well worth the effort.

Chapter 3

THE BOY FROM BARRA

Ian received an e-mail one day from a producer in London who wanted to discuss the possibility of a documentary about our work. We get contacted from time to time by television producers. Sometimes they just want an interview; other times they want our work to be the primary focus of a program. Ian was always extremely careful with media of any kind. He would usually say no to TV folks immediately. If not, with only a couple of exceptions, he would say no to them eventually.

I have been more open. Once I decided to focus on Western cases, I needed people to know about our work so they would contact us if their children started talking about past lives. Ian was always concerned about the work being sensationalized in the media, and the unfailing habit of producers to say they intended to make a serious film did little to alleviate that concern. Sensationalism, to some extent, can be in the eye of the beholder. I understand the coverage a program gives the work will be superficial to some extent—it's television after all—but I think such a show can have value despite its inherent limitations. I even did an interview for *Unsolved Mysteries* at one point. I knew it wouldn't challenge Edward R. Murrow for journalistic prestige, but at the time I was looking for American cases for a psychological testing study we were conducting. One mother, in quite a bit of distress, contacted me about her daughter after seeing the show, and I highlighted her case in my first book.

Even though Ian generally declined to participate in television productions or newspaper articles, he never objected to my involvement. At times, he would even help, supplying information or pictures from his old cases. When the e-mail came from the London producer, Ian, who had retired at that point, had our research assistant write back to decline. She added, however, that I was continuing his research and that, while I was open to the project, I wanted more details before deciding whether to participate.

The producer responded four months later. This is often a pattern with television producers. They approach us with great interest, disappear for a while, then contact us again, sometimes with a different person now leading the production. This tends to involve independent production companies who want to check out our interest before trying to sell a concept to a network. We understand this, so I never get too excited about any idea a producer is pitching. This producer explained that her production company had gotten swept up in another big project, which had required her to put potential future programs to the side.

A month later she wrote to say that Channel 5 in the UK had provided the production company she worked for, October Films, with some development money for a documentary about our work. It would air as part of a series on Channel 5 called *Extraordinary People*. We began discussing possible cases to be presented on such a program. This can be quite challenging. Production companies don't usually have the money to fly to Asia, where most of Ian's strongest cases are. Those cases are generally decades old by now anyway. A colleague of ours, a psychologist from Iceland named Erlendur Haraldsson, has investigated cases there more recently. I put the producer in touch with Erlendur, but the cost of a trip to Sri Lanka was more than Channel 5 wanted to pay.

Families in the West are often reluctant to go on television because they don't want people to know their child is talking about a past life. I discussed this program with several of the families of previous cases, so we had some potential leads. I then heard from Brenda Goldblatt, another producer at October Films. The first producer was now off the project due to maternity leave, so I started corresponding with Brenda about possible cases.

Time moved on, and eleven months after the initial contact, I had a phone conversation with Brenda. She said the network was committing a third of the project budget for a trip to film me investigating a new case. They wanted to be certain, however, that the outcome of the investigation would be positive. They were essentially asking for the impossible: for me to know that I would be able to confirm a child's claim about a past life *before* I confirmed it. As it turned out, the results from the case I eventually investigated were mixed, but it made for an interesting hour of television anyway.

The channel's wish for a guarantee of success wasn't the worst part. They also suggested that the program include a man who was "about to become famous" in England. He was a "baby whisperer." He would sit with babies and supposedly read their minds. The folks at Channel 5 wanted to see what he could glean about children's past lives. That didn't interest me in the least. The last thing I needed was for them to link another weird idea onto the topic of past lives, and I told Brenda that wouldn't work for me.

I think Channel 5 must have been talking about Derek Ogilvie, a professional psychic from Scotland who claims to read babies' minds. He was eventually the subject of an *Extraordinary People* episode. On that show, he failed two controlled tests, but he seems to have stayed plenty busy with his career since then.

I didn't hear from Brenda for a while, but in the meantime, October Films advertised in one part of Scotland for a family with a child reporting past-life memories. I learned later that though they got several responses, only one fit what they were looking for. Brenda e-mailed one day to say she had just had a fantastic call with the mother of a five-year-old boy named Cameron. He had been telling a consistent story for a couple of years. The family lived in Glasgow, but Cameron claimed he had another mother on Barra. Part of the Outer Hebrides off the west coast of Scotland, Barra is a remote island with little more than a thousand inhabitants. The family had never been there and had no connections with it. Brenda was preparing to meet Cameron and his mother the next day and wanted guidance about how to handle the situation. I emphasized that the key was to document as carefully as possible every statement Cameron had made. Only after that was done should he be taken to Barra. She said she would want me there for any trip to Barra, which certainly suited me.

Another three months went by because Cameron's mother pulled out of the project. The producers were ultimately able to get her back on board and were ready to proceed. In the hurry-up-and-wait fashion that seems to be the norm in television, they contacted me to plan a trip to Scotland as soon as possible. I would meet Cameron and his family in Glasgow, and we would then go together to Barra. The producers wanted to get the trip done in time for the end of that year's *Extraordinary People* series, but it ultimately didn't air until the next year. Their urgency meant we would need to go in February, a time, I soon discovered, when the Outer Hebrides tend to have inhospitable weather.

MEETING THE FAMILY

I took a red-eye flight from Washington to London and then a short flight on to Glasgow. I can never sleep much on planes and arrived a bit worse for wear, but after a short rest at my hotel, I received a call from Leslie, the director of the program, asking about a visit to Cameron's family. And so we went.

Cameron lived with his mother and his six-year-old brother, Martin, in a well-kept house. We sat down in their living room, and I started by talking with his mother, Norma. She said Cameron began talking about his Barra family when he was two and a half, and even more after he turned three. He would say, "I want to go to Barra to my other family," and he was quite adamant about it. He talked about Barra hundreds of times and daily when he was in nursery school.

He had given various details about his Barra family. He said his Barra father's name was Shane Robertson. In retrospect, I wish I had asked more about how Cameron had come to use that name because in the end, I wasn't sure we had the correct one. Leslie the director had told me in an e-mail a month before that she had just talked to Cameron's uncle, who remembered that when Cameron was about two and a half years old, he referred to his Barra father as Sean or Shane. By the time I met Norma, we also knew the Robertson part, but I didn't ask how long or how often Cameron had been saying it.

Regardless, he had been quite clear that his Barra father had stepped off the curb onto a road, didn't look both ways, and was hit by a car and killed. Cameron had talked about the car being either green and silver or greenish silver.

Cameron also talked a lot about his Barra mother. He said she had long brown hair but then got it cut short. He was crying one day and said his Barra family would miss him. He wanted his Barra mom to pick him up from preschool and said she would come and see him. He reported having three brothers and three sisters and said they played tag together. He once said one of his sisters was named Lindsay but at other times said he couldn't remember. He said the family lived in a white house that was much larger than the one he lived in with Norma and Martin. It had multiple toilets. Big stacks of boxes sat outside of it.

He talked a lot about things he did on Barra. He said he swam in rock pools and went down to the beach and played with friends. The family had a black dog with white on its chest, and he would take the dog out where there was lots of space. He said he used to go on holiday with his Barra family. At various times, he would say, "I used to do that in Barra." He once said he had used a black phone and described it as a dial phone.

Cameron never talked about being an adult and seemed to describe being a child who was a little older than he was himself. He never exactly said that he died. Instead, he said he "fell through" and came to Norma's tummy. The falling through seemed to involve a hole and the house he talked about. He said, "I was in Barra, and now I'm here."

Cameron talked about watching planes land on the beach at Barra. His mother hadn't known anything about that, but as we would soon find out, planes do in fact do that. Cameron talked about Barra so much that his brother, Martin, grew sick of it. Cameron would say, "Barra is real," but once when Martin was upset about it, told him, "If you want me to say Barra's not real, I'll say it's not real." He now wanted people to see that it was indeed real and was excited about our upcoming trip.

I then talked with Cameron. He was surprisingly forthcoming. We often have great difficulty getting the children to say anything to us about a past life. Not only are they uncomfortable talking to us as strangers, but many of the children have to be in the right frame of mind to discuss these things with anyone, even their parents. They usually do so during quiet, relaxed times. Cameron wasn't limited in that way, as he had talked about Barra in nursery school numerous times, and he talked to me as well, even with a camera rolling.

He said he used to run down and pick apples. He would play with friends in the family's front garden. He talked about crabs at the beach, saying he stayed away from them so they wouldn't nip him. He said his father's name was Shane Robertson and he had black, spiky hair. He had seen his father cross the road and then get knocked down by a car. He said it was a long car that was blue and green, this detail differing from his previous claims that the car had been silver and green.

Cameron told me his family lived in a white one-story house, but his mother said he had previously talked about stairs. The house was near the beach, and he had watched from it as planes landed. He said he had a sporty dog that was black and white and that it had a sore leg. He also described an orange cat. He said the boxes outside of his house had water and fish in them, though he had previously said he didn't remember what was in them. He also said he had been four years old when he fell out of bed and fell down a hole, leading him to come to his mother.

I was unsure what to make of that interview. Cameron seemed clear enough about the details, but some of them differed from ones he had given before. His mother had also said that his talk about Barra had calmed down for a while but now was back up. Being five and a half years old, Cameron was at the age when statements about past lives are typically tailing off. The resurgence in his might have been due to the increased focus on them from the television project; I was concerned it included new inaccuracies. Whenever a child's statements about a past life change over time, I'm inclined to put more stock in the earlier ones. Just as the accuracy of our memories for events in this life tends to decline with time, it may for past-life events as well, particularly since children seem to have less access to them as they get older. It was also possible that Cameron felt pressure to talk due to the cameras filming him and the doctor who had come so far to see him; perhaps this led him to give answers even if he wasn't sure he really remembered the details at that moment.

The TV folks had also talked with Cameron's uncle and the mother of one of his friends. I would have preferred to interview them myself, but in this situation it wasn't critical. When we get to a case only after the previous person has been identified, it's important to talk to as many people as possible who can confirm the statements the child made about that person before the identification. In Cameron's case, I was documenting his claims before anyone else attempted to verify them, and if we found someone whose life matched what he had said, we had a written record made beforehand.

Cameron's uncle remarked that Cameron had been consistent in his claims over the three years he had been making them. The friend's mother said Cameron had been adamant about his Barra family, talking about them over and over. She said her son told her one time that it's okay if you die because Cameron said you come back again as someone else.

At this point, we had established that Cameron had made claims about a life in Barra from a very early age. This seemed to go well beyond any kind of game. His Barra memories were clearly real in Cameron's mind. He talked with great emotion about a family and gave numerous details about life there. They included ones his mother didn't know. Even if Cameron had been exposed to information about Barra, latching onto it as the scene of a past life would have been peculiar, but he hadn't been exposed to any as far as Norma knew.

A TRIP TO BARRA

The next day, we headed to Barra. We took a commercial flight on a very small British Airways plane, and sure enough we landed on the beach, which served as the runway for the airport. The airport claims to be the only one in the world where scheduled flights use the beach as a runway. Cameron got off the plane telling his brother, "I told ya it was true." After we had walked from the beach into the airport building, he was beaming, saying he was happy to be back. The airport itself was so small that at the time, which was years after 9/11, it had no metal detectors. When we were boarding for our return flight, the airport staff simply checked our belongings by hand.

The TV folks then wanted us all to ride around for a while in the bus they had rented. Though Cameron said he recognized what he saw, there was no way to tell for sure, and the ride wasn't really productive.

More interesting were our activities the next day. Norma and I went to the island's heritage center to meet with the local historian, Calum MacNeil. I began by asking him about any accident in which a pedestrian had been killed as Cameron described. Calum said that he would know of any unusual deaths that had occurred, as drownings on the island back to the 1800s were still remembered. One man named Donald Mac-Lean had been killed by a bus in the early 1950s, but no one had been killed the way Cameron described his father dying.

I tried initially to withhold the name Robertson to see if Calum would give it spontaneously. I quickly discovered that the TV people had talked with him previously when they scouted the island, and he already knew we were looking for a Shane Robertson. What he had to say about one was not encouraging. He said that Robertson was a name that was only occasionally present on the island. There had been one man there in the 1930s. There was a Robertson family on the island at the current time, but the husband had moved there from elsewhere. And there were no Shane Robertsons at all.

Regarding other details, Calum said that for a person to watch planes land on the beach as Cameron had described, he would have to be on the northern end of the island, which Calum did not know as well as the southern part. He also said that toilets in houses only became common in the 1950s and '60s and only routine in the '60s and later. A house with multiple toilets as Cameron had claimed would have to be quite recent. He also said phones in houses were unusual when he was growing up but became more common in the 1960s. The phones available then would have been dial phones as Cameron described. Calum said that swimming in rock pools, as Cameron had reported, was very common. Cameron's story about Barra seemed plausible, except no family had been there that matched his description. Calum did mention that males named John were sometimes called Shawnie, especially if there was more than one John in the family. Shawnie was close enough to

Shane that it was a possibility, but the other details of the family still didn't fit for anyone.

At that point, it appeared we might be reaching a dead end. But then Calum called us later that afternoon—he had new information. When we went back to the heritage center, he told us he had done some more checking and learned that in fact there had been a family named Robertson who had lived on the north end of the island. They hadn't shown up in the records because they were from the mainland and had only holidayed on Barra. They were a shipping family who had a house on Barra in the 1960s and '70s, the time frame we were interested in. Their house, called the Sanderling, was a large white house very near the shore.

That was certainly a promising lead. The next morning, I went to the Council Records Department to look for any Robertsons I could find. Four marriages were listed, but there was little information that could be helpful. We went back to the heritage center yet again. Calum had continued to investigate. He had talked with one witness who said there were always children around the Sanderling. He had found the names of various members of the Robertson family there, though there wasn't a Shane.

The family had apparently spent quite a bit of time on Barra but didn't mix much with the locals. I did talk on the phone with a woman who said Mrs. Robertson had been a great friend of hers. Her memory seemed hazy, however, and she didn't even remember Mrs. Robertson's first name.

Calum had the name of a man who had supposedly known the Robertsons. We were able to get his address, and I went with Brenda the producer to talk with him. After a long ride, we got to his house and knocked on the front door. No answer. Brenda began looking for another way in. Being the intrepid journalist, she was preparing to climb a fence to get to the back door when the man came out on his porch proclaiming, "I don't know anything! I don't know anything!" And he didn't. The biting wind was whipping up as we stood outside cold and miserable and, worse, unsuccessful. As we climbed back into the van, Brenda's comment about the weather was a succinct "Bloody hell!"

While we were off on our wild goose chase, Leslie the director took Norma and Cameron to the Sanderling. They couldn't get inside, but they walked around the outside. As the video showed, Cameron seemed dumbstruck as he looked at the house. Though he eventually loosened up some, he was initially silent and downcast.

By the next day, the TV folks had talked with the current caretaker of the house. She agreed to open it for us and fortunately built a fire in the fireplace. As we walked through the house, Cameron acted as if it was familiar to him, commenting on parts of it. As we then sat around the fire, Cameron looked very sad. Norma asked if he missed his Barra mother. He nodded and leaned his head into her chest for a hug and comfort.

This kind of emotional reaction is something we often see in our cases. A five-year-old boy may not be able to express why he is feeling the way he is or even to know why, but Cameron was plainly experiencing feelings that were very real to him, ones of sadness and loss. Although these kinds of reactions may not carry the same objective weight as verified statements, such as his claim that planes used the Barra beach as a runway, that does not mean they are not important. They can be quite persuasive in their own way.

We have found that the emotions tend to travel with the more objective components of the cases. I developed a scale that measures the strength of each case. We code all of our cases on two hundred variables and enter them into a database. I picked out the items that would make one case stronger than another: the presence of birthmarks or birth defects that match wounds on the previous person's body, the number of statements the child has made that were verified to match the previous person's life, the behaviors the child shows that appear connected to the previous life, and the distance between the child's family and the previous person. The computer could then calculate a strength-of-case score for each case. I found that the amount of emotion the child showed when recalling the past life was strongly correlated with that score, meaning that children who showed more emotion were more likely to have the other features that make for a strong case. One aspect of greater carryover from a past life seems to be a continued emotional connection.

After the visit to the house, it was time for me to go home and for Cameron's family to return to Glasgow. We had found that a Robertson family had a house in the right location and with the right appearance. But the case still needed more investigation.

The TV folks continued the research. They contacted a genealogist who was able to trace the Robertson family. They were from Glasgow and owned the house on Barra for twenty-some years. She found contact information for one family member, a woman named Gillian who had spent holidays on Barra as a child.

Norma and Cameron visited Gillian. She confirmed the summers on Barra and said the couple who normally lived in the house did have a black-and-white sheepdog, as Cameron seemed to remember. There was no Shane Robertson. Though two men in the family had been named James (which can be referred to as Shamus), neither had been hit by a car. Indeed, no one in the family had died in any sort of car accident. Likewise, no children had died young, as Cameron's statements seemed to suggest he remembered doing.

Nonetheless, Norma said the family's trip to Barra had been therapeutic for Cameron. He was calmer about his memories after we took him to Barra, which she said was the best thing we could have done for him. Cameron said it was sad that his family wasn't there, but he was glad he got to see where he used to live. He seemed to have seen enough to validate in his own mind that the memories he had experienced were real. At the same time, he saw that the world had moved on. There was no family in Barra anxiously waiting for his return.

The trip was not as therapeutic for me as it was for Cameron. He had given accurate details of life on Barra, an island far away from his home, but some of the particulars he gave for his family appeared to be incorrect. This raised several possibilities.

A critic might conclude that perhaps Cameron saw something on TV about Barra and then imagined a life there. That, however, overlooks the emotional part. The memories that Cameron reported had great meaning for him. He didn't imagine these things on a lark; they were clearly very real to him. What could lead a child to create such things in his mind? And more to the point, was Cameron a child who would be likely to imagine a fantasy and then become convinced it was true?

One instrument that might be helpful in answering that question is called the Child Dissociative Checklist. It is a scale that was developed to measure dissociative behaviors in childhood. It includes simple behaviors such as daydreaming along with more worrisome items such as hearing voices and having two or more separate personalities that take control over the child's behavior. A parent or caretaker completes the checklist. Younger children tend to score higher than older ones, and a score of 12 or above indicates significant dissociative behavior, particularly in older children. Cameron scored a 1.

Studies of children who report past-life memories have found that most of them score quite low on the Child Dissociative Checklist, meaning they do not show significant signs of dissociating. When our colleague Erlendur Haraldsson studied children in Asia, he also included a scale measuring how suggestible individuals are. He found the children who had reported past-life memories were not more suggestible than other children. While skeptics might discount Cameron's claims as pure imagination, these children don't appear to be particularly fantasy prone.

For Cameron, there are a couple of other possibilities to consider. Several people contacted me about the name *Shane* after the documentary aired. Sean apparently means "old" in Gaelic, and the term for grandfather is *seanair* or *seanathair*. One woman wrote from the UK to say that her husband was from the Outer Hebrides, and his family referred to his father as Sean even though his actual name was something completely different. I'm not sure Sean would be pronounced there exactly like Shane, but it is evidently quite close.

The first name hardly matters, though, if the last name doesn't match. In this case, the only Robertson family we could find, though their life on Barra matched Cameron's statements in a general way, did not experience the specific events he had described. I was concerned we had latched onto the name too quickly. Cameron began by describing people and events he said he remembered, and it was only later that he gave the name Shane Robertson. He may have mistakenly put that name into his memories. In retrospect, perhaps we should have searched more intensely for a family whose father had been hit by a car and who had lost a child at an early age. Calum the historian had not heard of such a family, but he knew the southern part of the island better than the north, which is where Cameron's memories of watching planes landing on the beach would have taken place. We went with the name because it offered the potential of a definite verification, but that may have been a mistake. If Cameron was in fact remembering another family, that would mean his reaction at the Robertson house was perhaps from seeing a house similar enough to the one from his past life that he mistook it for that one.

Another possibility is that Cameron had memories from two past lives and mixed them together. His descriptions of Barra were accurate, but perhaps the particulars of his father being hit by a car came from another life. Though certainly not common, some children do indeed report memories from multiple past lives. This is easy to discern when the children clearly say they remember two distinct lives, but we don't know how many others may be unaware that the events they remember are actually from more than one.

SINGING AND DANCING

An example of a child with apparent memories from two separate lives is Ian's case in India of Swarnlata Mishra. Swarnlata first spoke of a previous life when she was on a trip with her family at age three. Passing through Katni, a city she had never seen before, she asked the driver of the truck they were riding in to turn down a road toward "my house." When the traveling group was having tea later, Swarnlata said they could get much better tea at her house nearby. After the trip, she began giving more details of a past life in Katni, saying her name had been Biya and that she was from the Pathak family. She gave details about her family's house, saying there had been four stuccoed rooms and the doors were black and fitted with iron bars. She said lime furnaces and a railway line could be seen from the house, and a girls' school was behind it.

Though Swarnlata's family moved around some, they never lived within a hundred miles of Katni. When Swarnlata was ten, she met a woman from Katni and said she recognized her from her previous life there. The following year, an investigator learned about her case. After gathering information from Swarnlata's family, he went to Katni and found that many of her statements (including all the ones I've given above) matched the life of a woman named Biya. She was from the Pathak family and had died nine years before Swarnlata was born.

When members of the Pathak family and Biya's marital family visited Swarnlata several months later, she appeared to recognize them, even though they arrived with a group of people and concealed their identities. Soon thereafter, Swarnlata and her family visited Katni and the places where Biya had lived after she married. Swarnlata recognized people and places Biya had known, commenting on various changes that had occurred after Biya died. Swarnlata continued to visit Biya's brothers as well as Biya's children, showing great affection for them.

Beginning at the age of five, Swarnlata also performed songs and dances, always one with the other, first for her mother and then in front of others as well. They were different from anything her parents had seen before. Swarnlata said they were from a different past life she remembered, a short one between the time of Biya's death and her own birth. She said she had been a girl named Kamlesh and she had lived in a place called Sylhet. (Sylhet was in East Pakistan, now Bangladesh, which limited Ian's ability to investigate Swarnlata's reports of her life there, and they remain unverified.) The songs were in a language other than Hindi, her native tongue. Her parents, not knowing what language it was, thought it might be Assamese, since Sylhet had been in Assam.

Ian's associate, Professor Pal, observed Swarnlata perform the songs and determined they were in fact Bengali, the predominant language spoken in Sylhet. He had her perform them three times so he could transcribe the words. He determined two of them were derived from poems by Rabindranath Tagore. The third was also in Bengali, but Professor Pal was unable to identify the source.

Professor Pal visited an institution founded by Rabindranath Tagore and watched a performance of one of the songs Swarnlata had shown him. He said the music was the same as Swarnlata presented it. The words she sang were very close to the original but with some changes. She said she had learned them from a friend named Madhu during her life as Kamlesh. Her performances suggested that Madhu had seen the songs performed and that Kamlesh then learned them from her imperfectly.

The name Kamlesh and the ones Swarnlata gave for other family members would be unusual for a Bengali family. She was unable to converse in Bengali and in fact had trouble recalling the words of the Bengali songs without performing the dances simultaneously. All of this suggested a life in Sylhet of a girl who, though from a non-Bengali family, had Bengali friends and learned the song and dance routines from one of them. Ian explored whether Swarnlata could have learned them in this life and thought it was improbable, if not impossible. He felt they were a paranormal part of her case.

Ian corresponded occasionally with Swarnlata and her family for the next forty years. At their last contact, Swarnlata, then married and a professor of botany, was writing to invite Ian to her son's wedding.

Swarnlata's family said she sometimes seemed to mix up the two past lives, though some of this may have been their own confusion about which life she was referring to. If Cameron's memories were perhaps fuzzier than Swarnlata's, it's plausible to consider that he was mixing up events from two different lives without realizing it. This would explain how he was so accurate about some aspects and so off on others.

The memories don't necessarily follow multiple past lives in a linear fashion. Ian noted that when children report memories of two lives, they usually talk more about the first one. The second one tends to be an unverified intermediate life that the child gives few details about. Thus, the memories are stronger for an earlier life. In contrast, in four of Ian's cases, the previous families said the deceased individuals had also remembered a past life themselves. The children in those cases, however, did not have memories of the earlier one.

Though memory is variable even in one life, the idea of a consciousness separate from our ordinary one again needs to be considered. The cases involving memories from multiple past lives seem more consistent with a separate consciousness carrying memories from different lives rather than one continuous stream of consciousness. Mind might be thought to have two parts, another one existing beyond the everyday one.

I am thinking of something along the lines of F. W. H. Myers's subliminal self. Myers was one of the founders of the Society for Psychical Research and a significant influence on William James, among others. He called the ordinary consciousness, the one above the surface, the supraliminal self. He imagined some sort of barrier or psychic membrane between it and the subliminal self. That membrane allowed information to move from the supraliminal ordinary self to the subliminal, but the reverse flow was much more limited. This was by necessity, so that the ordinary self could function in the physical world without being flooded by all the activities of the subliminal self. There could be uprushes, however, when material moved from the subliminal up into the supraliminal. These could cause problems but could also be positive, as Myers regarded genius and inspiration as arising out of the subliminal. Past-life memories might be thought of as subliminal uprushes, as material from the subliminal self that seeps into ordinary consciousness.

This subliminal self is more than what Freud called the Unconscious. Myers thought one part of each person was a soul that originated in a spiritual environment. It existed there even while embodied in a life in the physical world, and it continued there after the body's decay.

More about such things later, when I sketch out my view of what we can take from this research. As for Cameron, though he had some specific knowledge about Barra, his case is not completely fulfilling, largely because we were unable to find an individual whose life matched some of the details he gave. This limitation was not present in some American cases I would soon investigate, as the identity of the previous person in those was determined with certainty—to quite an interesting effect.

Chapter 4

THE THIRD JAMES

There has only been one case that I hounded the parents for years to study.

I first learned of James Leininger from a failed television program. I had agreed, against my better judgment, to be interviewed for a show about paranormal phenomena that ABC News was producing in collaboration with the ABC entertainment division. I initially declined, but one of their producers convinced me the segment on past-life memories would be "a serious look at this unusual occurrence." The producers had been in contact with past-life author Carol Bowman, who introduced them to two families with little boys who were talking about a past life. They decided to show one named James; his parents felt he was remembering the life of a World War II pilot shot down in the Pacific. The correspondent for the segment was Shari Belafonte. She and the crew were very pleasant when they came to our office to interview me about our research.

The show never aired. After viewing a tape that ABC eventually sent me, I was glad it didn't. It turned out to be a pilot for a show called *Strange Mysteries* that, as the introduction proclaimed, would explore "the supernatural, the mystical, the haunted." Along with "hair-raising memories" of past lives, it looked at topics such as animal psychics, séances, and psychic surgeries. The segment on past lives began with Shari Belafonte standing on a set in front of a spooky-looking house at night, complete with outdoor sounds such as a howl in the background. A haunted house intro was not exactly the "serious" approach I was hoping for.

The segment itself was okay as far as it went, and it included a look at James and his parents. He was a four-year-old boy with a fascination for airplanes. His parents reported that he began having terrible nightmares about a plane crash when he was two years old. By the time he was three, he had told them that before he was born, he was a pilot who flew from a boat. His plane got shot in the engine by the Japanese, he crashed in the water, and that's how he died.

Odd things for a little boy in Lafayette, Louisiana, to be saying. At that point, no one knew if what he was saying was true, if he was really remembering the life of an actual pilot. Though that uncertainty made the case less impressive at the time, the segment now exists as a record—made *before* a previous person was identified—of some of James's statements. This removes the possibility that his parents' memories of those statements later conformed erroneously to details of a deceased pilot's death.

Nearly two years after that interview was filmed, ABC's *Primetime* aired a different segment about James. This time the correspondent was Chris Cuomo, and he had conducted new interviews with James and his parents. The tone of the segment was more matter-of-fact, even as James's story had become more extraordinary. James's parents had now been able to verify much of what he had said. He said he had been a pilot named James on the boat *Natoma*, he had been shot down at Iwo Jima, and he had a friend named Jack Larsen. His father had discovered that a James Huston from the USS *Natoma Bay* had been shot down in the Iwo Jima operation. Another pilot on the *Natoma Bay* was named Jack Larsen.

That sounded like quite a case. I e-mailed Carol Bowman the next day and asked if she could find out if James's parents would be open to a visit from me. She responded a couple of days later to say that the parents were a little overwhelmed by the response to the *Primetime* piece, and at that point, they weren't interested in being interviewed. Not wanting to take no for an answer, I wrote to the Leiningers, explaining the potential importance of their story, since an American case in which a complete stranger, one who had been killed nearly sixty years before, was positively identified as the previous person was unprecedented in our studies.

Andrea, James's mother, called a week later. She was friendly and open in sharing details of events the family had experienced, and she agreed to have me study the case. After I e-mailed to thank her for talking with me, Bruce, James's father, e-mailed to say they would be happy to share what they had found. After a little back and forth, we figured out a date for me to head down to Louisiana to meet them.

I then received a call back. The *Primetime* piece had created quite a stir, and Bruce and Andrea were being advised to put off any interviews until they decided what they wanted to do with their story. Bruce felt their documentation of the facts of the case would hold up over time, so a meeting could wait. I had to accept that, not realizing it would be six years before we would sit down to discuss their experiences.

I sent periodic e-mails and letters to James's parents, with Bruce responding positively but never committing to a meeting.

In 2009, Bruce and Andrea published a book about James's case called *Soul Survivor*. I provided a blurb and sent a letter congratulating them on the book. Bruce responded, and at long last, we set up a time to meet. Bruce and Andrea hadn't wanted to get scooped on their own story, which I certainly understood, and since their book was out, they were open to sharing everything they had.

A MEETING AT LAST

By the time I flew down to Louisiana, James was about to turn twelve. Since these children usually stop talking about their memories by the time they are six or seven, speaking with James was unlikely to be fruitful. But that didn't concern me. I was most interested in what he had said before anyone identified James Huston as the pilot whose life he was remembering. Even if he were still talking about a past life, he might now have heard all kinds of things about this James Huston, and unless he showed knowledge about specific items he had not had the opportunity to acquire normally, his statements would provide little evidence that he was really remembering a past life.

I went to the Leiningers' house on a Saturday morning. Bruce and Andrea seemed like a typical American couple. Bruce worked as a human resources director, and Andrea, formerly a professional ballet dancer, worked both as a ballet teacher and as a résumé writer. Bruce came across as a no-nonsense kind of guy, completely cooperative and forthcoming but someone with definite opinions. He said that before everything started with James, he thought the idea of past lives was "pure baloney." To his credit, he was flexible enough for subsequent events to eventually change his mind. Even after all that had happened, his Christian faith clearly remained extremely important to him.

He made Biblical references at times, and he had worked to incorporate his experiences with James into his worldview of steadfast religious beliefs. Andrea was more open to nontraditional ways of thinking from the beginning, though she had no strong feelings about past lives.

I began with Bruce while Andrea and James were busy with other activities. We sat down at their dining room table. At one end of the room was a small bookcase filled with the research material Bruce had collected in trying to make sense of what James had said. The first noticeable incident in their story occurred when James was twenty-two months old. The family was living in Texas at the time, and Bruce took him to the Cavanaugh Flight Museum outside of Dallas. Before that, James would point at planes that flew overhead, but at the museum, he became transfixed. He kept wanting to return to the World War II exhibit. He and Bruce ended up spending three hours at the museum because James was so fascinated by those planes, and they left with a few toy planes and a video on the Blue Angels, the Navy's flight exhibition team.

The video became James's favorite object in the world, as he would watch it for hours at a time. I tried to find a copy, but it apparently never made its way onto DVD. Regardless, since the Blue Angels weren't formed until after World War II, the video could not be the source of the detailed knowledge James later displayed.

When James played with his toy airplanes, he repeatedly crashed them into the family's coffee table, saying "Airplane crash on fire." His parents are evidently tolerant, because Bruce has a picture that shows dozens of scratches and dents on the table. As if this weren't bad enough, whenever Andrea and James would see Bruce off at the airport as he was leaving on a business trip, James would tell him, "Daddy, airplane crash on fire." When he said that to his aunt before her flight, his dad gave him a stern reprimand.

A couple of months after the visit to the museum, the nightmares began. Andrea would find James thrashing around and kicking his legs up in the air, screaming "Airplane crash on fire! Little Man can't get out!" This was not just a one-time nightmare. James did the same thing night after night, multiple times a week. I talked with his aunt, Andrea's sister, after my trip to Louisiana. She emphasized several times just how disturbing these nightmares were to witness. Visiting James's family frequently, she saw a lot of them and said they were like watching someone in terror fighting for his life. They included blood-curdling shrieks from James as he kicked his legs up toward the ceiling, screaming about an airplane crash and a big fire and proclaiming, "Little Man can't get out!"

Several months into the nightmares, Andrea was reading James a bedtime story one night when he said, "Little Man's going like this" and reenacted his dreams, kicking his legs up in the air and saying, "Can't get out." She went and got Bruce to join them. This was a crucial event for Bruce. He had been dismissing James's nightmares as typical childhood events, but here was James talking about these things when he was wide awake. Bruce asked him what happened to his plane. James said it crashed on fire. Bruce asked him why, and James said it got shot. Bruce asked him who shot his plane. James, a little over two at the time, appeared exasperated and exclaimed, "The Japanese!"

A couple of weeks later, Andrea and Bruce had another bedtime talk with James. He said his plane was a Corsair, a fighter plane that was developed during World War II. He talked a number of times about flying a Corsair. Skeptics have pointed out that the Cavanaugh Flight Museum has a Corsair on display, arguing that James saw the plane there and the name stuck in his mind. Bruce told me that there wasn't one at the museum when he and James visited. There had been one, but it had crashed at an air show and was only replaced later. I looked into this and found out he was right. A Corsair on loan from the museum crashed at an air show in Wisconsin on July 29, 1999, six months before Bruce took James to the museum for the first time. I called the Cavanaugh Flight Museum and asked about the Corsair they have now. The woman there told me the current one was the replacement for the one that crashed in 1999, and that the museum obtained it around 2003. James did not see one on his trip to the museum and at twenty-eight months of age, knew the name from elsewhere.

Along with saying that night that he flew a Corsair, James also said he had flown off a boat. When Bruce asked if he remembered the name of the boat, James said, "*Natoma*." Bruce replied, understandably, that *Natoma* sounded Japanese. James, looking perturbed, said no, it was American.

Afterward, Bruce searched online for the word *Natoma*. After some effort, he found a description of USS *Natoma Bay*, an escort carrier stationed in the Pacific during World War II. Fortunately, he printed out the information and kept it, so we have a record of it. Each page of the printout has the name of the Web site as the footer, along with the date the pages were printed, 08/27/2000. Thus, we know that Bruce was searching for *Natoma* when James was twenty-eight months old. Some of the specifics of this case are dependent on the accuracy of Bruce and Andrea's memories, but not this. Unless you think this is an elaborate fraud, with this Christian couple in Louisiana faking a case of past-life memories despite potential derision by friends and neighbors, you have to conclude that little James did give the name *Natoma*. It's an unusual word, certainly not one people would typically give if they were trying to guess the name of a U.S. naval ship.

When Bruce and Andrea would ask James who the little man in the plane was, he would say "me" or "James," which at the time they took to be insignificant. A month or so later, he came up with another name. When his parents asked if anyone else was there in the dream with James, he gave the name Jack. They asked if he had another name, and he said Larsen. It was Jack Larsen.

In their book, the Leiningers write that Andrea then asked, "Was Jack James's friend?" and James replied, "He was a pilot, too." It seems obvious in retrospect that James was saying he was a pilot named James who knew another pilot named Jack Larsen. But at the time, Bruce wasn't seeing it that way. James was having nightmares. Beyond that, Bruce didn't know what he was dealing with, but he did know that James had given the name Jack Larsen. So he began looking for one. This search proved much harder than the *Natoma* one had been. He searched the World War II database on the American Battle Monuments Commission Web site on 10/16/2000. I have a copy of his search from that date, and I've since repeated it myself. It shows one Jack Larsen, one John Larsen, one Jack Larson spelled with an *o*, and four John Larsons. That site only includes those who are buried in the commission's cemeteries or listed on the Walls of the Missing. More important in this situation, it only lists casualties. The Jack Larsen from *Natoma Bay*, it turned out, had survived the war.

In my own online search, I went to the registry on the National World War II Memorial site. It combines four databases, though the one with survivors is unofficial and incomplete.

Searching for John or Jack combined with Larson or Larsen, I found nine listings for men who served in the Navy during World War II. Though that's an incomplete list, it at least gives some sense of how common the name was. Ships did not typically have a Jack Larsen on board. But *Natoma*, the one James had named, did.

Bruce wasn't searching for a living person because he assumed that James's dream, if it was a memory, was about being Jack Larsen. This was even though James kept saying he was "James" in the dream. I tried to sort this out with Bruce. He said he wasn't thinking James's dreams were memories of a past life. When Andrea's mother eventually suggested that, Bruce's initial response was, "That's bullshit." James said "me" or "James" was in the dreams with Jack Larsen, so Bruce apparently thought James was reporting a dream about a guy named Jack Larsen. Andrea, on the other hand, wasn't so focused on Larsen. She said she asked James thirty times what his name was in the dream, and he always said James. He said Jack Larsen was a friend he flew with. Given Bruce's confusion, it's possible that James's statement about their relationship may not have been as clear as Andrea now remembers it, but I do see how James referring to himself in the dream as "James" would be confusing.

Bruce's strong natural tendency to discount the possibility of past lives may also have contributed to his failure to understand what now appears to be the clear message of James's statements. Andrea's sister confirmed that for years, Bruce resisted past lives as an explanation for James's behaviors, because the idea conflicted with his Christian faith. Andrea grew frustrated with him about it, leading to disagreements at times.

THE SEARCH CONTINUES

About a month after mentioning Jack Larsen, James was just over two and a half when he gave another piece of information. Bruce had ordered a book, *The Battle for Iwo Jima 1945*, to give his father for Christmas. He was looking through it one Saturday morning when James climbed into his lap. They got to a place that showed a map of Iwo Jima on one page. On the other page is a photograph showing an aerial view of the base of the island, where Mount Suribachi, a dormant volcano, sits. James pointed at the picture and said, "That's where my plane was shot down." Bruce said, "What?" and James responded, "My airplane got shot down there, Daddy."

A week later, Bruce had his first talk with a *Natoma Bay* veteran. He found a reference to the *Natoma Bay* Association online and called one of the contact numbers. The man he talked to had served on *Natoma Bay* during the Iwo Jima operation. He remembered a pilot from the ship named Jack Larsen, but he didn't know what had happened to him. He said Larsen flew off one day and they never saw him again. Bruce assumed that meant Larsen did not return from a flight and became missing. At that point, he had confirmation that there was a ship named *Natoma Bay*, that it was at Iwo Jima, and that Jack Larsen had been a pilot on it. But he still had a long way to go to get all the puzzle pieces to fit together.

Andrea's mother sent her one of Carol Bowman's books. Despite his initial rejection of the possibility of past lives, Bruce read the book, and his resistance began to soften. Andrea contacted Carol. On Carol's advice, Andrea began talking to James about his nightmares right after he had them, and they quickly reduced in both frequency and intensity.

James also began talking more about his nightmares/memories when he was awake. This did not happen at predictable times and would often only consist of brief openings that didn't allow much follow-up from his parents. Soon after his third birthday, James began drawing pictures. He drew battle scenes with ships and planes over and over again—his parents report he drew hundreds of them. This kind of compulsive repetition is a phenomenon often seen in children who have survived or witnessed a major trauma; post-traumatic play, it's called. In this situation, how to distinguish post-traumatic play from the normal drawings of a boy who likes planes is not entirely obvious, but since the drawings occurred along with repeated nightmares about the same kind of scene, they suggest a child trying to work through a traumatic event. In James's case, this seemed to be an event from a past life.

James began signing the pictures, James 3. You might think this was because James was then three years old, but Bruce and Andrea say that wasn't why. When they asked him about it, he said, "I'm the third James. I'm James 3." I checked with each of them about this, and they were both definite that he said "I'm the third James." They have drawings he made after he turned four that still say James 3, so the 3 presumably does not refer to his age. What it may refer to is that James Huston was a junior. That would make James Leininger the third James.

Andrea's sister told me one story I had not heard from Bruce and Andrea. At one point when Bruce was frustrated with all the talk about a plane crash, he slapped a world map from an atlas down on a table and said to James, "Okay, where is Little Man's plane?" James pointed in the Pacific Ocean, and the adults all leaned down and saw that his finger was on a group of islands called the Ogasawara Archipelago. There in microscopic writing was the name Iwo Jima. Bruce confirmed the story and sent me a picture of the map. Spread across two pages and measuring twenty-two inches by seventeen inches altogether, it shows much of the globe. It's remarkable that a three- or four-year-old could identify any specific place on it, much less the location where events he was describing from a past life took place.

When James was three and a half, he talked one day about his plane getting shot. Bruce asked him where it had been hit. James immediately pointed to the front of the engine and said the plane had been hit right in the propeller. James was describing a plane with only one propeller, which was on the nose of the plane, so saying a plane had been hit in the propeller meant it had been hit in the front. Shari Belafonte pointed out on *Strange Mysteries* that none of James's toy planes still had their propellers on the nose, as James had apparently crashed them all until the propellers broke off.

Shari Belafonte and the *Strange Mysteries* crew arrived in Louisiana a couple of months after James turned four. Bruce talked with a producer about his search for Jack Larsen. After the filming, she sent him an e-mail (that I have a copy of) telling him to keep following the Jack Larsen lead. She said she had spoken with a contact at the Center for Naval History and asked about a Jack Larsen. That man found a John M. Larson, but there was no record of him dying in combat. That ultimately turned out to be the wrong person, but the e-mail does document that Bruce was looking for him long before he had everything figured out.

In September 2002, as James was nearing four and a half years old, Bruce attended his first *Natoma Bay* reunion. At the time, he didn't tell the veterans that his son had talked about a past life, saying instead that he was writing a book about the ship. He learned there that Jack Larsen, though not at the reunion, was still alive. He had not gone missing as Bruce had assumed; he had merely left *Natoma Bay* for another assignment. Bruce also learned that only one pilot from *Natoma Bay* had been killed during the Iwo Jima operation, a twenty-one-year-old from Pennsylvania named James Huston.

The statements I gave from James Leininger's talk with Bruce about Iwo Jima are from Bruce's *Primetime* interview with Chris Cuomo in 2004. At the time, he quoted James as saying, "That's where my plane was shot down." He now remembers James saying "That's *when* my plane got shot" rather than where. I don't expect every word to be identical this long after the events took place, but the difference is worth mentioning. James Huston's plane was shot down in the Iwo Jima operation but not actually over Iwo Jima itself. "When" would be more literally correct than "where" since the crash was during the Iwo Jima operation but not on Iwo Jima itself.

This seems a minor quibble even with "That's where my plane was shot down." James Huston might have said he was shot down at Iwo Jima if he could have told the story years later. The pilots of *Natoma Bay* made 123 flights in the Iwo Jima operation in the days before the start of the invasion and another fifty-two on February 19, 1945, the day the assault began. After that, its duties expanded as the battle to take Iwo Jima went on. As the Japanese were preparing a buildup of troop replacements and supplies, eight pilots from *Natoma Bay* took part in a strike against transport vessels in a harbor on Chichijima, an island about 165 miles from Iwo Jima.

The aircraft action report filed after the event notes the following: heavy antiaircraft fire put the planes under fire from both sides of the harbor. James Huston's plane was apparently hit by the fire as he approached the harbor entrance. None of the other pilots saw him hit, but his plane suddenly careened into a 45-degree glide and crashed in the water. It exploded and burned, and by the time two of the other pilots could get to the area, no wreckage of the plane was still afloat. Only a greenish yellow spot on the water marked where the crash had occurred. This happened on March 3, 1945, four days before *Natoma Bay* completed its work in the Iwo Jima operation.

Following the *Natoma Bay* reunion, Bruce visited Jack Larsen in Arkansas. Larsen was indeed very much alive. He remembered well the day that Huston was killed. He described the heavy flak the planes encountered as they arrived off of Futami-ko Harbor of Chichi-jima. Larsen didn't see Huston's plane go down, but he felt certain it had been hit by flak. Soon after Bruce got back home, *Natoma Bay*'s historian sent him a copy of the squadron war diary, which also described Huston's final flight. Bruce began to focus on Huston, seeing that all the pieces were starting to fit.

There appeared to be no way, however, to confirm James's claim that his plane had been shot in the engine. The aircraft action report from Huston's squadron stated that none of the ship's other pilots had seen his plane hit. But it turned out that the *Natoma Bay* crew wasn't the only source of information.

Bruce posted a query about Huston's crash on a Web site about Chichi-jima. Months later, he received a call from a veteran off another ship who had witnessed Huston's plane get hit. He had flown off USS *Sargent Bay*, which had also taken part in the attack. His plane had been hit that day, too, on its second run. On its first one, he had seen a fighter from *Natoma Bay* take "a direct hit on the nose," as he had written in an informal memoir.

Bruce talked to three other men who had seen Huston's plane get hit, and they all told the same story. One of them said Huston's plane was very close to his, and he and Huston actually made eye contact just before Huston's plane was hit in the engine and quickly engulfed by flames. Another one was interviewed for the *Primetime* segment. He said, "I saw the hit. I would say he was hit head-on, yeah, right on the middle of the engine."

All of this matched what James had described, as documented in the *Strange Mysteries* segment before the Leiningers knew anything about James Huston. In that interview, Bruce reported that when their James was two, he had nightmares about a plane crashing on fire and being unable to get out. Andrea said that one day, as James was playing in their sunroom, he told her, "Mama, before I was born, I was a pilot, and my airplane got shot in the engine and it crashed in the water, and that's how I died." Andrea also states on the segment that James had said his plane took off from a boat and that it was shot down by the Japanese. Shari Belafonte mentions Iwo Jima in the narration, saying James may have been one of the pilots during the battle there. That segment, along with the documentation that James said he flew from *Natoma*, produces a record that points to James having memories of James Huston's death.

James also said that Jack Larsen was there when his plane crashed. The aircraft action report for the day Huston was shot down includes a drawing of the paths each pilot took; Larsen's plane is shown next to Huston's. Bruce had found his man.

Along with the additional details that Bruce and Andrea report, we have definite documentation—from the *Strange Mysteries* interview and from printed records—of statements and behaviors from James Leininger, items that were recorded before James Huston was identified. Here are the statements and behaviors, compared to the details from James Huston:

James Leininger	James Huston
Signed drawings "James 3"	Was James, Jr.
Flew off Natoma	Pilot on *Natoma Bay*
Flew a Corsair	Had flown a Corsair
Shot down by the Japanese	Shot down by the Japanese
Died at Iwo Jima	The one *Natoma Bay* pilot killed in the Iwo Jima operation
"My airplane got shot in the engine and it crashed in the water and that's how I died."	Eyewitnesses reported Huston's plane "hit head-on right on the middle of the engine."
Nightmares of plane crashing and sinking in the water	Plane crashed in the water and quickly sank
Jack Larsen was there	Jack Larsen was pilot of plane next to Huston's

FAMILY FACTS

Andrea reports she asked James one day if Little Man had any brothers or sisters. James said he had a sister named Annie and another one named Ruth, or "Roof" as he said initially. He said Ruth was four years older than Annie, who was four years older than he was. Those details were correct for James Huston's family.

We do not have any verification of the conversation beyond Andrea's memory. When I first talked to Andrea after the *Primetime* segment aired, she told me she had made notes when James talked about these things so she could show them to Bruce, who was often away with his work. In the most disappointing part of my visit with them, I learned that after the Leiningers had written up the case for their book, Andrea either lost or threw out the spiral notebook she used to make notes. Though their book, along with the timeline and the detailed write-up they shared with me, relates the events, it doesn't constitute the same level of evidence that contemporaneous notes would have. Since verification is available for much of the story, the loss of the notes is certainly not a fatal flaw, but it would have been great to have them.

Regardless, Andrea eventually discovered through some clever detective work that James Huston's sister Anne was still alive. Andrea called Anne, who was eighty-four at the time, and then Bruce did as well. Afterward, Anne sent them some photos of her brother. Two of them solved a mystery for the Leiningers. Their James had talked repeatedly about flying a Corsair, as they described in the *Strange Mysteries* piece before James Huston was identified. This seemed to be incorrect for Huston. Bruce had learned that no Corsairs ever flew off *Natoma Bay*, and Huston had been killed flying an FM-2. The pictures Anne sent included two with Huston in front of a Corsair, one with a squadron and one by himself.

Bruce later discovered that before Huston joined squadron VC-81 on *Natoma Bay*, he had been part of a squadron, VF-301, that tested the Corsair for the Navy. The plane had been modified due to problems with landings. To test how well the modifications worked, the pilots in VF-301 took test flights with it, making 113 landings without difficulty. Bruce has several pictures of Huston with the squadron, and he talked to a veteran and the son of another veteran who served with him there. Following the testing, the Navy began using Corsairs, and Huston transferred to VC-81 on *Natoma Bay*. (An official history of the squadron documents that five fighter pilots transferred to VC-81 in October 1944, including ones from VF-301.) Though James Leininger was wrong when he seemed to say he was flying a Corsair when he was killed as James Huston, he was correct that Huston did indeed fly one. And getting to test an exciting new plane like the Corsair must have been quite memorable for Huston. Bruce talked with other pilots who had flown the Corsair, and they all felt demoted when they had to move down to more ordinary planes like the FM-2, the one in which Huston was killed.

Andrea reports that sometime later, she went into James's room one night carrying a glass of wine. James looked at the glass and said his father had been an alcoholic. His father would get drunk on liquor and tear up the house. When he was thirteen, the family had to put his father in the hospital for six weeks. His mother had to work as a maid during that time, and Ruth, his older sister, was "mortified." When their father got out of the hospital, Anne moved away.

At that point, though Andrea had talked with Anne on the phone, they hadn't met, and clearly James had no way of knowing such things. Andrea called Anne and asked her about what James had said. She confirmed the details. Her father had indeed gone into rehab. Ruth, who was working as a society columnist for the local paper, was definitely mortified when their mother had to work as a maid in the home of a family Ruth had written about. Anne, uncomfortable with their father when he returned, moved to their grandparents' home for her last year of high school.

I wanted to verify that phone conversation if I could. Andrea didn't have notes, but Anne was still alive. The Leiningers gave me her phone number, and I called her when I got back to Virginia. Unfortunately, I was asking a ninety-one-year-old woman to recall a phone conversation from more than five years before. She remembered that Andrea had asked about their father being an alcoholic at one time, but she couldn't recall any other specifics. Later, looking back through my file on

James, I came across a posting from July 2005 that Andrea made on the Reincarnation Forum, part of Carol Bowman's Web site. In it, she relates all the details of both of James's conversations about the family: the first one when he gave the names of Huston's sisters and the later one about their father's alcoholism. James was seven when Andrea posted that, so the events were relatively recent. And Andrea's memory of them had remained unchanged when I interviewed her five years later. Though that clearly wasn't perfect confirmation, it demonstrated consistency in the story over time.

SPECIAL KNOWLEDGE

James often surprised his parents with his knowledge of World War II planes. Around the time he turned two, Andrea bought him a toy plane and commented that there was a bomb on the bottom of it. James corrected her and said it was a drop tank.

During the filming of the *Strange Mysteries* segment soon after James's fourth birthday, one of the producers asked James about Corsairs, and he commented that they always got flat tires. The ABC crew then interviewed a military historian who stated that the Corsairs hit hard when they landed, often resulting in flat tires.

When James was six, Bruce made him a model of an FM-2, the plane Huston flew on *Natoma Bay*. James said something was missing. He said the planes had a small antenna on the side that people sometimes bumped into. The model didn't have one, but when Bruce researched the FM-2, he found that James was right.

Around the time James turned seven, he and his parents watched a History Channel program about Corsairs that showed footage of a Corsair chasing another plane the narrator called a Zero. James said it was a Tony, not a Zero. Bruce had heard of a Tony but couldn't identify one, certainly not as it shot across a television screen in old war footage. James explained the Tony was a Japanese fighter that was smaller and faster than a Zero. He also explained that it was called a Tony because the fighters were named after boys while the bombers were named after girls. When Bruce consulted the war diary for Huston's squadron, he found that the squadron had downed one Tony. Six of the fighters cornered the Tony and attacked it. The aircraft action report documents that Huston was the one who first spotted it.

James also seemed to remember details about life on *Natoma*. When he was five, Bruce was repairing some rotting trim when James picked up a sanding disc and said he had been looking for one of those. Bruce asked him what he wanted it for, and James said they never had enough records on *Natoma Bay*. Sanding discs do indeed look like old vinyl music records, and Bruce talked with a *Natoma Bay* veteran who said the ship had a record player with only one record.

Also when James was five, Andrea cooked meat loaf for the first time in James's life. When she told him what they were having, he said he hadn't had it since he was on *Natoma Bay*. He ate it up that night and said he had always enjoyed it on the ship. Bruce reports several veterans told him meat loaf was a regular meal there.

When James was six and a half, he attended his first *Natoma Bay* reunion. As he and Andrea were touring the museum, they came upon a five-inch cannon (which, despite the name, is a large object, as the five inches refers to the diameter of the projectiles it fires). Several veterans heard him say *Natoma Bay* had one of those, which it did. When one of them asked him where it was located, James correctly said on the fantail, which is on the back of the ship. Bruce isn't aware of any pictures of *Natoma* they might have seen that were taken from an angle that would show the cannon.

Also at the reunion, Andrea reports that she and James were stopped in the hotel hallway by Bob Greenwalt, a *Natoma Bay* veteran who had talked to Bruce on the phone but hadn't met any of the Leiningers. He asked James, "Do you know who I am?" James replied, "You're Bob Greenwalt." When Bruce asked him later how he knew that, James said he recognized Greenwalt's voice.

I wanted to get confirmation of the story from Greenwalt, so Bruce said he would contact him for me. After several unreturned phone calls, Bruce spoke to Greenwalt's wife and learned he was not doing well. In his late eighties, he was on oxygen with several severe health issues, so he was not available to interview.

When James was six, he was looking at the FM-2 model Bruce had made. He commented that they used to put oil in the drop tanks. The planes would drop them, and they would hit the ground and make a big fire. Bruce recalled a previous conversation with Jack Larsen. Larsen had been the assistant armament officer on *Natoma* and had described how they improvised napalm bombs by mixing napalm powder with gasoline in the drop tanks to form napalm jelly. They then included a hand grenade attached to a cable. When the tank was dropped, the cable would pull the pin of the grenade. If the timing was just right, the grenade would explode as the tank hit the ground, producing a remarkable explosion. Bruce hadn't read about that anywhere and knew of no way James could have learned about it.

PAST BEHAVIOR

The children in our cases often show behaviors that appear connected to their reports of past-life memories. This most often relates to the occupation of the previous person. That was certainly true for James. His fascination with airplanes seems to have been passionate to the point of being obsessive. Along with the countless toy planes he had, when he was four, he used an old car seat and pieces from various objects to create a play cockpit in the closet of Bruce's home office. Bruce would hear him pretending to be a pilot, and then James would come tumbling out, pretending to parachute after his plane had been hit.

Another behavior James showed was a ritual after getting into his car seat. He would raise his hands over the top of his head and pull them down to just over his ears. He would then move his right hand down in front of his face to his chin. His parents figured out the ritual when they took James to an airshow when he was three and a half. James was able to sit in the cockpit of a Piper Cub, where the pilot had his headgear with the earphones and microphone attached. Andrea watched James put on the headgear and use the same motions to put the earphones on his ears and the microphone in place at his chin that he used in his car seat ritual.

When James was four and a half, he and his parents visited some of Andrea's family in Dallas. They went to a community pool, where James and his cousin began playacting. James pretended to shoot at airplanes and talked about shooting "the Japs." After a short time, Andrea called him over and told him he shouldn't say that. She said the war was over anyway and we beat the Japanese. James was momentarily stunned and then became ecstatic, jumping up and down and screaming in celebration. Andrea told me about this the first time we talked on the phone, which was a year and a half after the incident occurred. Her sister and Bruce still remembered it well six years later. It was embarrassing for the adults but funny, and it was another demonstration of the emotional connection that James, like the children in many of our cases, had to the events he appeared to remember from long before.

When I was finally able to talk to James as he neared his twelfth birthday, those emotions were no longer apparent. As is usually the case, the memories themselves seemed to be gone by that age as well, though James had hinted he might still have some he could talk about when he was older. I was able to see him away from the actual interview, both at home and when we all went out to dinner. He presented as a typical boy his age. He was well-spoken but not formal or pseudo-mature. He could become silly at times when he was joking around, and he was close to his parents, but not too close. All in all, he seemed to be a fine young man, certainly not weird or disturbed in any way.

HEAVENLY MEMORIES

When James turned three, he got his first G.I. Joe and named it Billy (or Billie, as it turned out). When he received his second one that Christmas, he named it Leon. Two Christmases later, when he was five and a half, he received his third, which he named Walter. These G.I. Joes were his buddies, and he took them everywhere. He played with them in the tub and slept with them at night. Andrea's sister remembers him naming one immediately after he unwrapped the package. His parents were particularly struck by the names Leon and Walter, as they aren't common ones for a young child to use. When they asked him why he chose those, he told them because that was who met him when he got to heaven.

Ten men from Huston's squadron aboard *Natoma Bay* were

killed before he was. The names of three of them were Billie, Leon, and Walter. James's parents even discovered that the hair color for each of them matched the hair of the G.I. Joes. Billie Peeler had brown hair, Leon Conner had blond hair, and Walter Devlin had red hair, as did their respective G.I. Joe namesakes.

The day after James's comment about meeting them, Andrea brought up the topic again and asked James if there was really a heaven. When he said yes, she asked where it was, and he spread out his arms and said, "It's right here." She asked what it looked like, and he said it was the most beautiful place in the world.

Andrea asked him if there is really a God, and James said yes. She then asked if God is a man or a woman. I would guess that a lot of very young children from Protestant homes would imagine God as a man with a long white beard, perhaps looking like Charlton Heston, sitting on a throne. James's answer was that God is not a man or a woman; he is whoever you need him to be at the time.

Andrea also asked him if everyone comes back. James said no, that you get to choose. You don't have to come back. You can, but if you don't want to, you don't have to.

James also had an interesting story to tell about coming back. When he was four and a half, he was "helping" Bruce rake leaves one day when Bruce hugged him and told him how happy he was to have James as his son. James responded that when he picked Bruce he knew he would be a good daddy. Bruce asked what he meant, and James said that when he found Bruce and Andrea, he knew they would be good to him.

Bruce asked James where he had found them, and James said Hawaii. The three of them had gone to Hawaii that summer, so Bruce told James he didn't find them there because they were all there together. James said no, it wasn't that time; it was when only Bruce and Andrea were there. Bruce asked James where he had found them, and James said it was at the big pink hotel. He added that he found them on the beach when they were eating dinner.

Bruce and Andrea had indeed gone to Hawaii before James was born. They stayed at the Royal Hawaiian, a large pink hotel on Waikiki Beach, a different section of Honolulu than where they visited with James. That was their first week of trying to get pregnant, and Andrea had just gone off birth control pills. Bruce and Andrea finished their time there with a nighttime dinner on the beach. Though James was not conceived in Hawaii, Andrea was pregnant within a couple of months.

All in all, this is quite a remarkable case. Though I might have been able to corroborate parts of it more if I could have studied it sooner, it still stands up very, very well. In fact, I have trouble coming up with an ordinary explanation for it. You may say it was all a coincidence, but if so, it was one heck of a coincidence.

James appears to have had memories of James Huston's life. This little boy showed knowledge of events from the Pacific in World War II, and not just knowledge, but emotions from those events and the trauma of being killed there. Even so, he is now a happy, thriving young man, the trauma seemingly behind him. The third James is enjoying his new lease on life.

Chapter 5

HE CAME FROM HOLLYWOOD

Our office received a "To Whom It May Concern" letter one day from a mother in Oklahoma named Cyndi. She said she was hoping we might be able to help her solve a case of possible reincarnation. Her five-year-old son, Ryan, had been having memories of what his parents believed was a past life. She explained that she grew up in a Baptist church and that her husband was the son of a Church of Christ minister. They had never been taught to believe in reincarnation. They were ordinary people; her husband was a police officer and she was a county clerk deputy. Ryan was not ordinary and had lately had some extraordinary stories to tell.

About a year before, Ryan began talking about going home to Hollywood. He would cry and plead for Cyndi to take him home so he could see his other family. When this preschooler was playing, he would often shout "Action!" and begin to direct imaginary movies. His parents didn't take all this very seriously until a few months later, when he began having nightmares. He would wake up grabbing his chest and saying he couldn't breathe. He said that when he was in Hollywood his heart had exploded.

One night, Ryan said he wanted to tell Cyndi what it was like when you die. He began describing an awesome bright light and said you should go to the light. He said everyone comes back and that he knew Cyndi before. He claimed he picked her to be his mother.

Since Ryan seemed to be struggling with the memories, Cyndi went to their public library and picked up some books about Hollywood, in hopes that Ryan might see a landmark that would trigger memories that were more specific. As they looked through them, Ryan became excited when he saw a photograph of Rita Hayworth. He said he knew her and that she used to make "those ice drinks." He later said she called them Coke floats.

They came across a picture in another book from a 1932 movie called *Night After Night*. Ryan got excited again, and as he looked at the men in the photograph, he pointed to one of them and said, "Hey Mama, that's George. We did a picture together. And Mama, that guy's me. I found me." The photo shows six men, with all eyes on the two in the middle having a confrontation. The second man Ryan pointed to is on one side, wearing a black bow tie like the rest, along with a bowler hat and an overcoat.

The book didn't list the people in the picture, so Cyndi was unable to identify the man Ryan said he had been. She did verify that the first one was George Raft, a film star in the 1930s and '40s, primarily in gangster movies.

Ryan said he had been friends with a cowboy who was in the movie. He said this cowboy had a horse he did tricks with. He also said the cowboy had made cigarette commercials. With a little work, Ryan's parents discovered that an actor named Gordon Nance was in *Night After Night*. He later changed his name to Wild Bill Elliott. He starred in Westerns and was also a spokesman for Viceroy cigarettes.

Ryan described a scene in the movie that involved a closet full of guns. Later that night, Cyndi found *Night After Night* on YouTube. She saw that there was indeed a scene that included a closet full of guns. She pointed out that Ryan was only five and had never even seen a black-and-white movie, much less this one.

He also reacted to a picture of Marilyn Monroe, whom he called that Mary lady. He said he had been at a party one night and tried to talk to her. He laughed and said one of the studio guys punched him in the eye. He said you couldn't even get close enough to talk to her because those studio guys wouldn't let you. He said he liked being Ryan but he liked living in Hollywood, too. He said he had made films and that he had lived in a big house with a swimming pool outside.

Cyndi wrote that the most bizarre thing Ryan had done was describe some events that happened while she was pregnant with him. It was a story he shouldn't have known anything about, but he said he saw it all from heaven. She didn't provide any other details in the letter, but I learned more later.

Cyndi said she was writing because she really wanted help in identifying the man in the picture Ryan had pointed to. She said that he told her he was starting to forget about his life in Hollywood. That made him sad, but at the same time he just wanted to be Ryan. Cyndi finished by saying that Ryan was a great little boy and she wanted him to have answers to the questions he cried about at night.

We hear from American parents frequently, usually by e-mail these days but sometimes by postal mail as well, but it's rare to get that much detail from them. And having a picture of an unnamed man whom the child says was his previous identity is unprecedented. I watched *Night After Night* on YouTube myself. There was in fact a scene involving a closet full of guns. I also found the one that the photograph in the book was taken from. The problem was that the man Ryan said he had been had no lines in the movie; he was playing a henchman of one of the other characters. That would make identifying him quite a challenge. The movie itself is notable for being Mae West's film debut and includes a classic Mae West line. A hat check girl sees her and says, "Goodness, what beautiful diamonds!" West responds, "Goodness had nothing to do with it, dearie."

I wrote back to Cyndi and asked if she and her family would be open to a visit from me. She responded that they would greatly welcome a visit or any kind of information I could give them. She also mentioned that she had started keeping a journal about Ryan, which meant we would have documentation of the things he said.

Ryan didn't want to talk to anyone about Hollywood because he was afraid people would think he was crazy. I explained to Cyndi that it would be fine if Ryan didn't talk to me, but I was hoping he would warm up after I was there awhile. I said she could let him know I didn't think he was crazy, I was just really interested in the life he had described to Cyndi.

We exchanged e-mails leading up to our meeting. In one, Cyndi reported that Ryan said the reason he had to come back was that he didn't spend enough time with his family in his last life; he worked so much that he forgot that love was the most important thing. In another, she said Ryan had told her he had nightmares about a man they called Senator Five, whom he described as the nastiest villain that ever lived. He talked about an agency and going to a graveyard in New York with a buddy that worked for the agency. A week later, Cyndi said Ryan was resisting going to kindergarten because after he would tell the class about Hollywood and the agency in story time, kids would make fun of him when he said the stories were real.

I wasn't sure what to make of some of the stories myself. Ryan's talk about the agency and Senator Five sounded rather fantastic to me. The stories reminded me of a case a colleague of mine investigated in which a young boy gave startlingly accurate details about a man who had lived hundreds of miles away. He would then get wound up and begin talking about race car drivers and various make-believe topics. It was difficult to tell what counted as past-life report versus pure fantasy.

Ryan also talked some about Broadway. He began doing a tap dance routine and said he remembered it when he heard some music on a cartoon that sounded like the music he used to tap to. He said he had done it with two buddies. He hadn't taken formal lessons but had taught himself.

When the family was packing for a vacation trip to Branson, Missouri, a month before we met, Cyndi told Ryan he could dress up when they went to see a show there. He responded, "Oh Mom, I hate auditions." The play they went to was a variety show that included a tribute to veterans. During a piece on Pearl Harbor, Ryan became very emotional. He booed a clip of Franklin Roosevelt, and when his dad got on him about it, he turned to his mother and said, "Daddy doesn't know what an idiot that man is." Halfway through, he began muttering about "the damn Japs." He cried during the presentation and stood applauding at the end.

In planning my trip to meet the family, I would be taking along a small flip camera to record our interview. A month before I received Cyndi's letter, I had gotten a phone call from a television producer named Russ Stratton, who was interested in making a program about our work. Such calls are usually from producers hoping to pitch an idea to a cable network. In this case, Russ said that A&E was already on board. And one of the producers involved in the project was Doug Liman, the director of films such as *The Bourne Identity* and *Mr. and Mrs. Smith*. The plan was to have a first-rate director reboot an A&E series from the 1990s called *The Unexplained*.

Russ seemed sincerely interested in our work, and I agreed to participate in the project. The plan was to show a re-creation of a previous case, but in discussing recent ones, I mentioned that I was preparing to go to Oklahoma to meet a family. One of the producers sent me a camera to film the interview. The understanding was that the footage probably wouldn't be shown on television and certainly not without the family's permission. Even so, the producers thought the opportunity to have an initial interview on film was too good to pass up, and at the very least, it would give them a better understanding of what was involved in studying a case.

A VISIT TO OKLAHOMA

I flew to Oklahoma to meet Ryan and his parents early on a Saturday afternoon. Cyndi was warm and pleasant. Her husband, Kevin, a police officer, seemed out of central casting for an Oklahoma lawman with his stocky build, his closely cropped hair, and Southwestern drawl. He definitely did not come across as someone you would expect to promote the idea of past lives. Ryan, at that point three months short of his sixth birthday, was initially reticent as these children tend to be. He was clearly fascinated by the camera, which I set up on a small collapsible tripod the producers sent, and Kevin had to admonish him several times not to touch it. Ryan didn't touch it, but he sure wanted to.

We sat at the kitchen table to talk about the things Ryan

had said. He had usually made his statements at night, often right after his bath. His personality seemed different at times, with a more mature vocabulary. He might talk about his memories three days straight and then say nothing about them for three weeks. He initially would only talk to Cyndi about them but lately had begun talking to Kevin as well.

Cyndi had sent me a copy of the notes she was keeping. She was sometimes adding entries on a daily basis. This meant his comments were fresh in her mind when she recorded them. He once said, "I used to be big; now I'm little." Another time, he said, "I liked it better when I was big and I could go wherever and whenever I wanted to go. I hate being little." Cyndi reported that if Ryan saw a shot of the Hollywood Hills on television, he would always say, "That's my home. That's where I belong." At one point, he said, "I just can't live in these conditions. My last home was much better."

He made various statements about family. He said his mother had curly brown hair. He talked a lot about a sister, who was three years younger than he was. He talked about a daughter and said her mother liked to put her hair in either pigtails or a ponytail. At other times, he also talked about three children. He wasn't sure if they were his children or not, but he remembered bringing elaborate coloring books to them. He said he drove a green car, while his wife had a nice black one.

Ryan talked about traveling a lot. During the family's vacation to Branson, they were walking along the brick streets downtown when Ryan became excited and pointed to a small café with outdoor seating. He said the place reminded him of when he went to Paris. They had restaurants outside there and fountains in the middle of the street, and he went and saw the big tower. He asked Cyndi what the tower was called, and when she told him the Eiffel Tower, he said, "That's it, Mom. I have been to the Eiffel Tower in Paris." Cyndi asked if he had really been there, and he said, "Yes, Mommy, I have been to China, Paris, New York. When are you going to listen to me? I have seen the world."

One day he walked into the kitchen and asked if he and Cyndi could dance together. He said, "Mommy, I can't wait until I get big again and I get to go on those big boats, wear fancy clothes, and dance with all the pretty ladies. That's how you see the world, Mommy, from a big boat." He mimicked dancing what appeared to be a waltz and said that dipping was his favorite part of dancing on a ship.

He talked about visiting China and said you had to learn to use chopsticks there because they didn't have silverware. He said you got good at it if you wanted to eat. He also talked about Chinatown a lot and said they had the best food there. When he was in preschool, he asked one day if the family could go eat at a place where they used chopsticks. His parents took him to a Chinese restaurant. He loved the food, eating all of it while refusing to use silverware. Kevin said he was amazed at how proficient Ryan was with his chopsticks.

Ryan talked about how much he hated cats. He told Cyndi one time that when he was living in Hollywood, he tried to help an injured cat that didn't know him. The cat scratched him "something awful" and there was a lot of blood. He then showed her where the scratches had been on his arms. He said another time that he got his daughter a watchdog but she didn't like it.

One day, Ryan said he wanted to watch cartoons all day. Then he said, "Mom, just get me a Tru Ade." She said, "What?" and he replied, "I mean a Dr Pepper." She did an online search and found that Tru Ade was a noncarbonated soft drink that came in orange and grape flavors. It seems to have been made from the 1940s through the '60s or early '70s. Cyndi showed Ryan a picture of an ad for Tru Ade, and he laughed and said, "You can't get that stuff anymore. Now I just drink Dr Pepper."

I asked about Ryan's agency talk. I was thinking that Ryan was referring to being a secret agent, and Cyndi seemed to think so, too. But he never quite said that. He had said he worked in an agency where people changed their names. And he talked a lot about Senator Five and what a mean person he was. He once asked for a map of the United States. He pointed to New York and said that's where they went to see Senator Five. He said they saw him in a graveyard there. A few hours after pointing out New York as the place they met, Ryan told Cyndi that if she could find Senator Five on the computer, he could pick him out. He said he could pick him out because he saw his face at night when he was asleep.

Parents have often told me there is a distinct difference in their children when they are describing their purported past-life memories compared to when they are engaging in make-believe. They tend to be more serious and matter-of-fact talking about a past life. I asked Cyndi if there was any difference in how Ryan talked about the agency part compared to how he talked about Hollywood. She said he did seem a little different. I gathered he showed more sadness and longing talking about Hollywood, whereas he was more energetic discussing the agency.

Ryan also made comments about little things, often when triggers in the environment such as smells or music seemed to stir his memory. Cyndi was patting Ryan's leg one afternoon when he said it reminded him of when he was in Hollywood and he used to get "those skin burns." Cyndi asked if he was talking about sunburns, and he said he used to get them all the time in Hollywood.

One night at bedtime, Ryan said he didn't want to go to sleep because he didn't want to have nightmares again. He cried for about thirty minutes, saying repeatedly, "Mommy, I'm homesick. I'm just so homesick." Another time, he said he used to live somewhere with the word *Rock* or *Mount* in it. A while after the interview, I told Cyndi about my search for towns with those words in the name, but she said Ryan had talked as if Rock or Mount was part of the street address.

Ryan also made comments about his time between lives. At one point, he said he went somewhere after he died, but not to heaven. It was a waiting place. Another time, he said he saw his parents from heaven. He said he picked his mother but not his father and that he came back to take care of her.

When Ryan's parents married, they decided they would only have one child because Kevin already had two from his first marriage. Cyndi very much wanted a daughter. Ryan came over to Cyndi one night and asked why she had thought he was going to be a little girl. When she asked him who told him that, he said no one told him and that he saw it from heaven. He said, "This doctor guy did a test and told you I was a boy. You got mad and said he was wrong. You just knew that I was going to be a girl. Mommy, it was Daddy's birthday, you went to a restaurant afterward to eat and you cried for a very long time."

Cyndi reports everything happened just as Ryan said. She had always regretted the way she acted that day. It's hard to imagine she had ever told Ryan about it.

After the interview, we went out to dinner, which Kevin insisted on paying for even though I could put it on my expense report. He and Cyndi came across as completely sincere, and there seemed no chance they had put Ryan up to saying the things he had. The question remained, however, whether

Ryan had made it all up. He did appear to have an active imagination. The emotion he attached to his claims, however, indicated this was more than just make-believe to him.

The only way to answer the question was to find out if the man in the picture had done the things Ryan described. But figuring out the identity of a nameless face from a 1930s movie seemed a nearly impossible task. I looked into posting the picture on the Turner Classic Movies message board. That would be a real long shot, but I thought it might be worth a try.

A POSSIBLE IDENTIFICATION

A couple of weeks after my trip to Oklahoma, I received a telephone call that changed the search. One of the television producers called because the family they had planned to film for their program had backed out. So they wanted to use Ryan's case instead. This would mean that the television folks could use their resources to search for the man in the picture, which greatly increased our chances of identifying him. The question was whether Ryan's family would agree to participate in a program for television.

I e-mailed Cyndi and explained the situation. I made clear that it was completely up to them to decide if they were comfortable with the prospect of Ryan's story being told on television. If they decided they didn't want to do the program, that would have no effect whatsoever on our interactions. Cyndi wrote back to say she had watched a show about psychic children a few nights before and all she could think about was how much Ryan's story could help some other family going through a similar experience. She said she was interested in letting Ryan do the show, but she would want it done with them in shadow with different names.

Cyndi also asked if the producers would want to film Ryan

in Hollywood. I responded that they probably would if she and Kevin were agreeable to it. She said the reason she asked was that Ryan had been saying repeatedly that he was going to go to Hollywood for three days and that he was going on a big airplane. She reported he had been talking about that even before the family knew anything about our initial visit being filmed.

After one of the producers called and talked with Kevin, he and Cyndi decided they better tell Cyndi's father, the one remaining grandparent who didn't know what Ryan had been saying. They were surprised when he actually took the news better than the rest of the family; he said he had seen things on television about other children like Ryan. Ryan was excited about this news, saying his grandfather didn't think he was crazy and he could tell him about Hollywood now.

As Cyndi was getting Ryan ready for bed that night, she told him, "Ryan, you do know that you are not that man in the picture anymore. We just want you to be Ryan." He responded that he was not the same as the man in the picture on the outside but that on the inside he was still that man.

Cyndi e-mailed the following day to say that Ryan didn't want the interview done in shadow and didn't want his name changed. He said that what he was going through was real and that if his parents believed him they wouldn't want to be hidden. This put Cyndi and Kevin in a tough spot. They live in a small town, and they were concerned about what people would think of them if they went on television with Ryan's story. Cyndi's family was opposed to the idea, but since she didn't want Ryan to think she and Kevin were ashamed of him, she e-mailed the producer and told him they would agree to be on the program with their identities unconcealed.

The television crew then visited Ryan's family. Russ Stratton, the first producer I had talked to, was not part of the group.

He was still overseeing the project, but a separate team had been hired to do the filming. Cyndi reported that Ryan had a great time with them, and he enjoyed playing with all the equipment they brought in. The crew filmed interviews with the family. They showed Ryan the book with the picture from *Night After Night*, and they captured him on camera pointing to the man he had identified and saying, "That one's me."

The television folks then thought they might have figured out who that man was: an actor named Ralf Harolde. But they based this solely on their sense that Harolde looked like the man in *Night After Night*. After a little research, I wasn't so sure. Just looking at pictures of him, I wasn't convinced he was the same person. I also saw that Harolde's real name had been Ralph Wigger. When I found Wigger in the census records, I saw that he appeared to be an only child, even though Ryan had talked at length about having a sister. Records from when Wigger was one, ten, and twenty years old listed no siblings.

The television people decided to take Ryan to Hollywood to see what he might remember, making his prediction about taking a trip there come true. I wanted to accompany his family, but we couldn't get my schedule to line up with the director's. Since the crew was under time pressure, the group went ahead with the trip without me.

I received a report from Cyndi the day the family got back home, even though they arrived at two in the morning. The trip proved to be rather arduous for Ryan and his parents. It began with another interview in the hotel room. The problem was that while the television folks were trying to capture Ryan saying something extraordinary on camera, he was getting annoyed because he wanted to see Hollywood. He did enjoy the hotel, the Hollywood Roosevelt Hotel, which was built in 1927 and hosted the first Academy Awards two years later. He made comments to Cyndi and Kevin about remembering it, but only when he was away from the cameras.

The film crew took the family to see two homes where Ralf Harolde had lived. He had apparently lived in quite a few places, and they went to the first and last of his houses. Ryan showed no reaction at all. At the last one, Kevin asked him on camera if any of it looked familiar to him, and Ryan said no. Cyndi said that Ryan did recognize the house of Wild Bill Elliott, the actor from *Night After Night* he said he had been friends with. She also reported he loved seeing the ocean and said he used to bring his girlfriends there.

I responded to Cyndi that since Ryan showed a reaction to Bill Elliott's home but not Ralf Harolde's, I was again wondering if Harolde was the right guy. Ryan continued to talk about past memories, not only about Hollywood but New York as well, saying he played the piano there.

A BREAKTHROUGH

Six weeks after the family's trip to Hollywood, I received an e-mail from Russ Stratton, the producer overseeing the television project. It said, "Please call when you have a moment . . . we've had a breakthrough on Ryan's case . . . we've definitely identified who the actor was." That got my attention. When I called Russ, he gave me the update. He had been dissatisfied with the Hollywood trip. When he found out from the crew that their only method of identifying Ralf Harolde was to look at pictures, he was really dissatisfied.

Russ hired an archival footage consultant named Kate Coe to try to find out who the man in *Night After Night* was. She initially figured the job would be easy. Once she learned the details, however, she changed her mind. As she said on *The UneXplained*, she thought, "Oh, wait a second. It's an uncredited extra. It's some guy in a hat!" She sent the photo from the movie to other researchers, and no one could identify him.

Eventually, she went to the library of the Academy of Motion Picture Arts and Sciences, probably the largest film library in the world. She got all the material she could find on *Night After Night*. Most of it involved the stars of the movie. Then she spotted a picture of the man she was searching for. He was looking into the camera with a long cigar in his mouth and a bowler hat on his head. The caption of the picture just gave the name of the movie and the stars. On the back, however, was this description: "What the well-dressed racketeer will wear. Marty Martyn, playing a racketeer in Paramount's 'Night After Night', with George Raft, Constance Cummings, Wynne Gibson, Mae West and Alison Skipworth, gives a demonstration of underworld sartorial excellence."

What's odd is that Marty Martyn is listed in the credits at the end of *Night After Night* playing a character named Malloy, even though the man Ryan pointed to had no lines in the movie. This initially made me unsure if that man really was Marty Martyn, so I watched the movie again. No one is called Malloy in the film, and none of the other actors look like Marty Martyn. Only two characters wear bowler hats, the man Ryan pointed to and his boss, who was played by an actor named Bradley Page. The actor Ryan pointed to had to be Marty Martyn.

We finally had a definite name to go with the face. With a little work, Russ's team was able to find Marty Martyn's real name and some basic facts about his life. He only had one biological child, a daughter with his last wife. Russ's team was able to identify her and find her phone number. Russ called her up. Some of their conversation is on the *UneXplained* program that eventually aired. Russ tells her a little of the story and finishes by saying they think the man Ryan identified was Marty

Martyn. The daughter responds, "That's my father! Is this some kind of a joke?" She was understandably skittish about the whole thing. Russ sent her an e-mail detailing how they had found her, with the thread involving a family history volume in the New York Public Library as well as various online databases.

While she was processing it all, we had work to do. Now that we knew the identity of the man in the picture, I could test Ryan to see if he would recognize people Marty Martyn knew. In the Asian cases, families have often conducted informal tests that were completely uncontrolled. As Ian wrote, the tests often occur with a large group of people around. Someone asks a leading question such as, "Do you see your wife here?" When everyone looks expectantly at the previous person's widow, the child can hardly fail to point out the correct person. There have been exceptions, such as the case of a little girl in Sri Lanka named Gnanatilleka, who was presented various individuals from the previous person's life (and a couple of people whom the previous person never met) and asked if she knew the person. She correctly identified the ones the previous person knew and gave some details about them she could not have known based solely on their appearance.

In Ryan's case, it made no sense to try to bring in people Marty Martyn had known, since he died in 1964. But I could show Ryan pictures. Russ's group had photographs of a number of people from Marty Martyn's life, and at my request, they also produced similar ones of people Marty did not know.

With those in hand, I made a trip back to Oklahoma to see Ryan's family again, this time with a film crew joining me. Russ had taken over the hands-on work of making the program, and he and his producing partner, Amy Hobby, led the team. Before going, we told Cyndi that the man in the picture was not Ralf Harolde, as the previous production crew had guessed, and that we now knew his actual identity. We didn't tell her the correct name because I wanted to make sure the recognition tests were untainted. I didn't think she would start madly researching Marty Martyn's life, but I wanted to make sure that possibility didn't even exist. This was quite difficult for Cyndi. Russ had told her about a few items, which likely only tantalized her more, but no identifying details. She said she guessed Ryan's statements must be pretty accurate if all of us were flying to Oklahoma so quickly, but after dealing with this thing for months, she was dying to know all the facts.

Ryan was initially happy to hear that the man in the picture had been identified and that he wasn't Ralf Harolde. But in the days leading up to the visit, he became skeptical about being filmed again. He said he didn't want to deal with the television crew. He felt they had tried to make a joke out of him in Hollywood. He wanted to know why they didn't listen when he said he didn't know Ralf Harolde's houses and why they lied to him about what his previous name had been. He said it wasn't fair that he didn't remember his name.

Cyndi explained that a different film crew would be coming this time. She told Ryan that the crew didn't mean to lie about the man's name and that everyone makes mistakes. He was adamant that he would not cooperate. Cyndi told me she was hoping she and Kevin could get Ryan prepared before we all arrived that weekend. I told her we would certainly be gentle and that with luck, Ryan would warm up after a while.

When we arrived, Ryan was definitely in a mood. He had been sleeping poorly and was clearly uncomfortable about us being there. Russ apologized to him for the way the filming had gone in Hollywood. Even so, this was a lot to ask of a child.

Ryan had just turned six years old, which was a particularly difficult age for what we were trying to do. It can be hard for a child that young to cooperate with any activity for a significant period, especially as people are filming him. At the same time, he was getting a little old for the past-life images to still be prominent in his mind.

Adding to the difficulty was the frustration Cyndi was feeling because we would not tell her the name of the man in the picture. Ryan could feel her frustration, which she was then taking out on him when he had trouble cooperating. She said later she was acting so harshly toward him that she should have been filming an episode of *Supernanny*.

We attempted some recognition tests. Russ and his team had collected pictures of various people Marty Martyn had known. I may have made two mistakes when I showed Ryan the pictures. I showed him lineups, four pictures at a time, in which only one was someone Marty Martyn had known. This might have been too much for a six-year-old to take in. I could have shown him one picture at a time, some being people Marty knew and some not.

The other possible mistake was that when I showed him the pictures, I simply asked him if any of the people looked familiar. I was being intentionally vague in hopes that if Ryan did recognize anyone, he would then give details such as the relationship Marty had to the person. Ryan said later he didn't understand what I was asking. He thought I was asking if the pictures looked familiar rather than asking him to identify specific people.

Our initial tests did not go well. It was clear Ryan didn't want to do them and was pointing at pictures randomly. We took several breaks and after a while decided to give up for the day. We all went out for dinner at a barbecue restaurant and had a good time. When we got back to the house, Ryan said he wanted to try some more pictures. I was concerned he might be too tired, but he was clear that he wanted to try.

We sat at the kitchen table. I showed him pictures of four women, one of whom was Marty Martyn's last wife. When I asked Ryan if any of them meant anything to him, he pointed to the picture of Marty's wife. I asked him about her, and he only said that she looked familiar.

I told Ryan and his parents that I thought I might know who Senator Five was. I showed him pictures of four men. He pointed at one and said with apparent certainty, "That's Senator Five." I asked him, "Are you sure?" and he answered, "I'm sure." Ryan had said that he met Senator Five in New York. I checked records and found that New York didn't have a Senator Five but did have a Senator Ives. Irving Ives was a U.S. Senator for twelve years in the late 1940s and the 1950s. I thought Five and Ives sounded so much alike that a young child could easily mix them up. Senator Ives was the man Ryan pointed to.

I then showed Ryan pictures of four young men, one being Marty Martyn, who were all carrying tennis rackets. Ryan picked up the picture of Marty and said he remembered it, that it looked familiar. I asked him how, but he only said it was familiar. I then explained that this was the same man as the one in *Night After Night* Ryan had pointed to, only he was younger in this picture. Though this recognition may not be as impressive as the first two since Ryan had already seen the picture of Marty from *Night After Night*, Marty did not look identical in the two pictures, as they were taken at different angles and at different ages.

I tried a couple more tests. Ryan began missing again, and

we called it a night. We left some of the pictures, and Ryan looked at them with Cyndi after we were gone. One was a family picture that included Marty's last wife, his five stepchildren, and an inset of his daughter. Ryan pointed to the older stepdaughter and told Cyndi, "I used to talk to her and give her advice. She never wanted to listen to me. She had no respect." He didn't like the pictures of Marty when he was older, the bald pictures with the glasses as Ryan called them. He preferred the ones where he looked "young and handsome."

The next morning, we met again. I had typed out a list of four names. One was Marty Martyn. The others were similar kinds of names—John Johnson, Willie Wilson, and Robert Robertson—because I didn't want Ryan to pick Marty Martyn simply because that name stood out. I had Kevin read the names, since I knew the correct one. As he read the others, Ryan said no after each one but was silent on Marty Martyn. He then pointed to Marty Martyn's name, and when Kevin asked him, "Marty Martyn?" he confirmed his choice.

MEETING MARTY'S DAUGHTER

After that visit, Ryan was confused at times about Marty's daughter. People explained that she had grown up. He said he thought she was still little and that everyone was making up the idea that she was now old. He said he remembered her being not much bigger than he was then and that he really didn't think he had been gone that long.

Cyndi had hoped that solving the mystery of the man in the picture would enable Ryan to put his past life behind him. As she said, she kept praying the memories would diminish and Ryan could just be happy. At one point, he told her, "Mommy, I just want to be me, not the old me." He then got angry and said to tell Marty's daughter he didn't want to meet her. "She got old. Why didn't she wait for me?" He got upset and walked off.

Ryan eventually came around. He predicted he would get a chance to meet Marty's daughter. He planned on loving her instantly because he said you can feel love and it doesn't go away. Marty's daughter remained unsure about participating in the project. Russ sent her a DVD with some of the footage of Ryan and his parents and eventually met with her. After being assured that all of this was on the up and up, she agreed to a meeting. She would talk with me and meet Ryan, but she did not want to be filmed.

Since Marty's daughter lived in the Los Angeles area, the meeting meant another trip there for Ryan. Russ's team had arranged for us all to meet at a small house. Ryan's family dressed up more for the meeting than they had for previous events, which I thought was a way of showing respect for Marty's daughter and an appreciation for her willingness to meet. Despite Ryan's intention to love Marty's daughter instantly, he seemed intimidated by the experience. As the family walked into the house, Cyndi asked Ryan to introduce himself. Ryan stepped forward and shook hands with Marty's daughter. She said, "Hi Ryan, nice to meet you." Without responding, Ryan turned around and went back to Cyndi. He was standoffish for the rest of the meeting.

Afterward, Ryan told Cyndi that Marty's daughter wasn't like he thought she would be, that her energy had changed. Cyndi responded that when people grow up, they change. Ryan said, "Same face, but she didn't wait on me. She changed; her energy changed. I don't want to go back. I want to always keep this family." His response was like those many of the Asian children have shown following similar meetings. The intense longing for the previous family they have repeatedly expressed often dissipates (though not always) when they see that the people they have talked about have aged as their lives have gone on. The children's memories have been validated, but they also see that things have changed.

MARTY MARTYN'S LIFE

Before Ryan met Marty's daughter, I sat down with her to review his statements. She had only been eight years old when Marty died. She had fond memories of him, but there was a lot about his life she didn't know. In fact, she hadn't been aware of the existence of one of his sisters, who died at an early age.

Even so, between her memories and the records Russ's team had unearthed, we were able to piece together a picture of Marty Martyn's life, and we could compare it to Ryan's statements. In most of our cases, people have tried to see if a deceased person could be identified whose life matched the statements the child had made. Here, there was only one guy that Ryan could have been talking about, because he had pointed to him in a picture. We weren't trying to see if there was anyone whose life matched Ryan's statements; we were looking to see if Marty Martyn's did.

What we found was that though Ryan was off on some of the details, a lot of what he said was correct for Marty Martin. It had seemed unlikely that an extra with no lines would have danced on Broadway, had a big house with a swimming pool, and traveled the world on big boats. But Marty Martyn did.

Marty was born in Philadelphia in 1905. Ryan had talked a lot about a sister and also mentioned another one, and Marty had two sisters. His mother had curly brown hair, as Ryan had said. Ryan was right about dancing in New York, as Marty and one of his sisters went to New York to be dancers. He danced in various reviews on Broadway, and his sister became a well-known dancer there.

Marty then moved to Los Angeles, having a life in Hollywood as Ryan had described. He began as an extra as well as a dance director. He then became a Hollywood agent, not the secret agent kind but a talent agent. He set up the Marty Martyn Agency, where he had notable clients such as Glenn Ford. Ryan had talked about people changing their names with the agency, which would certainly be true for a talent agency. Marty had several connections to Rita Hayworth, and his daughter confirmed he probably did know her. He may well have interacted with Marilyn Monroe as well, as his wife's family knew her.

Marty was a big sunbather, getting sunburns as Ryan had mentioned. Ryan said he used to take girlfriends to see the ocean, and there are pictures of Marty with young women on the beach. He enjoyed going there and watching surfers, which Ryan had said as well.

Marty was married four times. He became quite wealthy, and he and his last wife enjoyed an upscale lifestyle. Ryan said he had driven around Hollywood in a green car and that his wife drove a nice black car. Well, Marty's wife didn't actually do the driving, but they had a custom-made Rolls-Royce that was presumably a nice car. Ryan remembered an African American maid, and Marty and his wife had a number of them. Ryan said he owned a piano, and Marty had pianos in his house. The family lived in a fine house with a large swimming pool, as Ryan had described. Ryan said his address had Rock or Mount in it. And Marty Martyn's last house, that fine home with the big swimming pool? It was located at 825 N. Roxbury.

Ryan said one time that when he was a little kid, his family didn't have a TV in their house; no one did. He said he was so excited when he got his first TV. That statement, while accurate for Marty, was quite general. It would have been true for anyone in Marty's generation, but I still found it notable that a six-year-old child would understand that people in that era didn't have televisions.

As Ryan had reported, Marty and his wife traveled the world. Marty's daughter doubted he ever went to China as Ryan had said, but there was a Chinese restaurant in Hollywood he really enjoyed. Marty and his wife did go to Paris a lot. In fact, his daughter showed us a picture of her parents in Paris. Ryan had spoken of traveling on a large ship and doing a dance like a waltz on it. Marty and his wife had traveled to Europe on the *Queen Mary*, where dancing took place.

Ryan had said that Theodore Roosevelt was the best president ever, and he had booed Franklin Roosevelt. Marty was a Republican, and his wife was a major Republican as well. As for politicians, Marty did indeed meet Senator Ives from New York. His daughter said she had a photograph of the two of them together. Though there is no evidence that Marty felt the animosity toward him that Ryan demonstrated toward Senator Five, the two men definitely met.

Ryan had talked about having a daughter as well as interacting with other children, but he was unsure if those were his. Marty had one biological daughter along with five stepchildren, and he did indeed have a difficult relationship with his older stepdaughter as Ryan had said. One item that was probably incorrect was that Ryan said that his wife enjoyed putting his daughter's hair in pigtails or a ponytail. If Marty's wife did, it was when his daughter was too young to remember it. She did say that her father hated cats, as Ryan had described. Ryan said he gave his daughter a watchdog that she didn't like. Marty Martyn got his family a dog—though since it was a Yorkshire

Terrier, it wouldn't have been much of a watchdog—and his daughter didn't like it. Ryan talked about bringing coloring books to a group of children. Marty's daughter said he brought her a lot of coloring books.

Ryan had asked for a Tru Ade to drink. Marty's daughter didn't remember seeing him drink those, but she did say that he liked Orangina soda, a similar drink. Ryan had said he loved bread in his last life, and at another time said he loved blueberries. Marty's daughter confirmed that rye bread and bagels were among her father's favorite foods, and he also loved fruit.

Ryan said he had been a smoker. Marty smoked cigars and had a monogrammed cigarette case. Ryan said he had died when his heart exploded, but this was apparently incorrect for Marty. He died on Christmas Day in 1964. He had leukemia, and his daughter reported he was in the hospital when he died of a cerebral hemorrhage. Ryan would wake up grabbing his chest and saying he couldn't breathe. Marty's death was apparently unwitnessed, so there is no way of knowing precisely what he experienced when he died. Ryan did say that he died in a room with numbers on the door, which was likely true for Marty's hospital room.

Some of the other things Ryan talked about did not match Marty Martyn's life. For example, he talked about a father who had raised corn and then died when Ryan was a child in his last life. There were many other items, scores of details, that we were unable to either prove or disprove for Marty, since our sole sources of information were public records and a daughter who was only eight when he died.

Even so, many of the details Ryan gave did fit the man he pointed to in the picture, who had a much more exciting life than anyone could have guessed a movie extra would have. Though that might seem like strong evidence for reincarnation—and it is—there is another factor in Ryan's case that complicates matters.

A CHILD PSYCHIC

Ryan has had a number of incidents in which he seemed to demonstrate special knowledge. He told Cyndi one night that there were supposed to be three babies in her family. When she said she didn't know what he was talking about, he repeated that there were supposed to be three babies in her family and said a baby was born in the first week of July but not on the first day as Cyndi was. The baby came early; he was supposed to wait to be born. He decided he wasn't ready to come back yet so God didn't make him stay. When Cyndi again said she wasn't sure what he was talking about, Ryan started to cry and asked her to call his grandmother so he could ask her about the third baby. He said his grandmother had been very sad and that she really thought she was going to get to take that baby home. Cyndi told him it was too late to call that night but she would call the next day.

Cyndi's mother had indeed had another baby besides Cyndi and her brother. With her first pregnancy, the baby was born premature and died minutes later. His birthday was July 8, and Cyndi stated with certainty that her mother had never talked about the baby around her grandsons. When Cyndi told her mother what Ryan had said, she started crying.

Another time, Ryan, Cyndi, and Cyndi's mother were shopping out of town when they took Ryan into a walk-in hair salon to get a haircut. Ryan told the woman cutting his hair that he wanted her to use her red scissors, the ones that had special meaning to her. She asked how he knew about those. He told her he was psychic and could see them in his mind. She then took a black case out of her drawer, unzipped it, and pulled out a pair of red scissors.

Ryan would sometimes touch people's faces with his fingers and say that he needed to feel their energy. He did that to his grandmother and told her she was going to get chicken pox. Two weeks later, she came down with shingles, an illness produced by the reemergence of the varicella zoster virus that causes chicken pox.

Ryan came by Cyndi's office with his dad one day on their way to see a movie. Cyndi's phone rang, and Ryan picked it up and handed it to her. When the man started talking, Ryan reached down and pushed the button to end the call. Cyndi, no doubt exasperated, asked Ryan why he had done that. He responded that the guy had the wrong number and was an idiot. The man called back, and sure enough, he had the wrong number and did act thoughtlessly, arguing with Cyndi about having the wrong phone number.

On Ryan's first trip to Los Angeles, Ryan told Cyndi as their plane was landing that they would have white cars when they got to Hollywood. When the traveling group got to the rental car lot, they received a white car and a white van.

Cyndi took Ryan to the store one night to pick out some pool toys to take with him to his grandparents' house the next day. He picked out water blasters, and Cyndi said he could get two, one for him and one for his cousin. Ryan insisted he needed three, but Cyndi told him two was enough. On the way to his grandparents' house, Ryan said his grandfather would break his cousin's before he even got to use it. Cyndi responded that Ryan's grandfather probably wouldn't be in the pool. When they got to the house, Ryan's grandfather was in shorts and ready to swim. Before Ryan's cousin arrived, his grandfather accidentally broke the water blaster Ryan had gotten for him. They needed a third one, as Ryan had said.

Cyndi e-mailed me the day after Father's Day to say that a couple of weeks before, Ryan had gone on and on about wanting to buy Kevin a watch. When Cyndi told him Kevin already had a watch, Ryan insisted he would need one by Father's Day. When Kevin came home from work on the morning of Father's Day, he explained that during a fight with a drunk man that night, his watch had been broken.

Cyndi went on to say that later that day, she and Ryan went shopping so Ryan could get his grandfather a present. His grandfather is a diesel mechanic, and Ryan said he wanted to get him a special wrench. He said he wasn't sure if his grandfather would need a wrench that he didn't have or if his would get broken, but he knew his grandfather would have to buy a new one.

A few days later, Cyndi e-mailed again to report that Ryan's grandfather had to leave a job site the previous day before he was completely finished with his work. He asked a man who worked for him to drive his truck home while he rode with someone else. The man didn't put all the tools back in the toolboxes, and when Ryan's grandfather got home, he noticed that they were scattered on the back of the flatbed truck. He thought some of the tools had probably fallen off onto the road, and sure enough, by the end of the week, he had bought some new wrenches.

Cyndi also said in the Father's Day e-mail that Ryan told his grandmother that day that she was going to hurt her back and have to go to the chiropractor. Four days later, Cyndi e-mailed again to say she had just gotten off the phone with her mother, who had been in the kitchen putting up dishes when she turned wrong and threw out her back.

That August, Cyndi reported that Ryan was predicting who his teacher was going to be for the second grade. He told her he had seen the list in his mind and knew which teacher he would be getting. When Cyndi told him they would need to wait until the next week to find out, he wanted to bet an Xbox on it. Cyndi wouldn't bet him, which turned out to be wise because the following week she e-mailed me a picture of the post card he had gotten from his new teacher, the one he had predicted.

I called Ryan's grandmother and confirmed with her all the incidents that involved his grandparents. I might be able to write off one or two of these, but with so many happening, Ryan appears to have some psychic abilities. (I realize this is a controversial area, but if you're this far into a book on past-life memories, I hope the possibility of extrasensory perception isn't too much of a stretch.) This raises the question of where Ryan's knowledge of Marty Martyn came from. Was it all memories, or did his psychic abilities lead him to know about events he didn't personally experience? And did seeing the picture of Marty Martyn connect Ryan with information about his life that Ryan then interpreted as memories? For that matter, were some of the details that Ryan gave that didn't match Marty Martyn part of a flood of information about other people's lives that Ryan perceives because of his psychic abilities?

Most of the children we study have not demonstrated special knowledge about anything other than the life of one deceased person. And the details they report are not just objective information but seem to be memories from the viewpoint of that person. When Ryan cried about missing his old life, he was showing an emotional connection to material that he felt he had experienced, not just events he knew about. Still, a special case like Ryan's may give us clues that knowledge is not always completely isolated in each of our brains, as he seemed to have access to information he could not have gained through the usual functioning of his brain. There may be a more diffuse field of knowledge rather than just individual points where it resides. Similarly, it's easy to think of past lives in a linear fashion, with separate souls moving from one life, to another, and then another in a straightforward progression. The reality may be more complicated than that, as I'll discuss at the end of the book.

RYAN'S POSTSCRIPT

After the meeting with Marty Martyn's daughter, I had a plane to catch. The TV producers took Ryan and his parents to some of the sites Marty Martyn had known. They went by Marty's last house on Roxbury, the one with a big swimming pool. Unfortunately, the house had recently been torn down, and a new one was being built in its place. Ryan seemed okay with that. They visited the building where the Marty Martyn Agency had been. Ryan walked all the floors of the building and even asked if he could stay longer. He also enjoyed going to an apartment complex Marty had stayed in, as well as the Beverly Hills Hotel, where Marty once had a bungalow. The next day, they went to the beach, and Ryan enjoyed playing in the sand and watching the surfers.

Following that trip, Ryan's talk about Marty Martyn's life became infrequent unless something reminded him of it. Cyndi found that he did much better with showers in the morning than baths at night, which often seemed to bring out longings for the past. She was pleased that he had learned to live more in the here and now. Ryan did continue to say he wanted to see Marty's youngest stepson. He wanted to tell him that he knew he had turned out well. He was sorry he hadn't visited him during his trip to Hollywood, but he didn't know where the man lived.

Cyndi was understandably nervous about the television program that would show Ryan's case, both about the program itself and about people's reactions to it. But everything turned out well. *The UneXplained: A Life in the Movies* aired on April 30, 2011 (on the Biography Channel rather than A&E as originally planned). Cyndi, Kevin, and Ryan all felt that the producers did a great job with it.

Cyndi soon received a telephone call from a Baptist minister, after someone lent him a copy of the program. As it happened, Kevin had previously had conflict with him. Cyndi saw him occasionally because he was the pastor of one of her co-workers, and he had always been pleasant. He called to tell Cyndi not to let anyone keep her from helping Ryan reach his full destiny. He said how inspiring Ryan's story was and how it proved that God could do big things. He told Cyndi he couldn't wait for his wife to get home so she could watch the program, and he planned on showing it at the next Bible study meeting at his church. Cyndi was so stunned that this Baptist minister, who had clashed with her husband, was calling to offer her encouragement about Ryan's past-life story that she could barely speak. Though not everyone Cyndi and Kevin knew was as open-minded, most people's reactions were positive.

While Ryan continues to make spiritual remarks and to have psychic impressions, his talk of Marty Martyn has stopped almost completely. Six months after *The UneXplained* aired,

Cyndi walked in his room one night to find that he had taken down all of his wall decorations, including his iron Eiffel Tower and his pictures of New York. He told her it was time to just be a regular kid. He wanted to know if his dad could paint his room and if they could get him some Oklahoma Sooners bedding and sheets. His parents were thrilled.

Chapter 6

FAMOUS NAMES FROM THE PAST

We occasionally get e-mails or letters from people who think they were famous in their past lives. This typically begins when they feel a connection to a historical figure. They then see things they have in common with that person, such as interests or abilities, or parallels in their lives such as both having absent fathers or attending boarding schools or traveling to other countries. At times, hypnotic regression or a "past-life reading" is involved in identifying the famous individual. Even though many of the people who write us do not claim to have specific memories from their famous past, they have become convinced nonetheless that they were significant historical figures.

Some of these people are leading quite accomplished lives and show no signs of being mentally ill or excessively fantasy prone. Even so, we view such reports with great skepticism. First, there is the matter of statistics. The number of people from the past who were famous is such a small proportion of the overall population that it is unlikely that any given living person was someone famous in the past. It is beyond unlikely that among our correspondents would be five people who were Mary Queen of Scots, five who were Thomas Jefferson, two who were Amelia Earhart, and so on. But as a correspondent once remarked to Ian, if we've all had past lives, *some* of us must have been famous before.

Apart from the statistics, there is the more critical issue of how to tell who someone might have been in a past life. Unless the person has actual memories that can be verified, trying to identify the past life of a present-day individual becomes little more than pure speculation. We have always focused on young children because they are the ones who spontaneously report specific memories of previous lives that can be checked for verification. For famous figures, the young age is important for another reason. The most impressive memories in our cases involve information the children could not have learned through normal means. It would be very difficult for an adult to recall details of a famous figure's life that he or she could not have known before but that could nonetheless be verified as accurate.

The reports about famous past lives almost always come from adults, but there have been occasional exceptions. Ian and two colleagues wrote a paper about seven purported past-life cases that involved deception or self-deception. In one of them, a man in Turkey greatly admired John Kennedy. Just before his son was born in 1965, he had a dream in which President Kennedy came to his house and said he wanted to stay with him. The man then named his newborn son Kenedi, giving it a Turkish spelling. When Ian interviewed the man as his son was turning two years old, the father reported that the boy would say he was President Kennedy when he was asked his name.

Ian was amused by the case but thought no more of it until an associate happened upon it again when Kenedi was nineteen. At that point, his father said that Kenedi had added that he lived in America, was married, had two children, and was rich, facts that were presumably common knowledge every-where. Kenedi himself was convinced at age nineteen that he really had been President Kennedy. Ian, on the other hand, thought the case illustrated how a parent can unintentionally impose an identification of an admired individual onto a child.

I now present two cases in which the previous person was famous, or at least quite well known, in his day. These two have distinct differences from the ones above. They involve very young children whose statements about being a previous indi-vidual were completely unexpected by their parents. Though any claims regarding a famous person may raise certain con-cerns, these two cases also include some intriguing features.

HE CAME FROM HOLLYWOOD TOO

A month after Ryan's mom first wrote me, I received an e-mail from another mother, named Jennifer. She began by saying, "Forgive me for contacting you out of the blue." (No forgive-ness was necessary since I'm always looking for new cases.) She said she had been searching the Internet for days for some-one who might be able to help her.

She thought her son Lee, who was three and a half years old, might be remembering a previous life. She said things had begun about a year before with small incidents such as argu-ments over his middle name and the date of his birthday. From there, he had made other comments. Jennifer said he was grow-ing increasingly angry because she wouldn't take him to his "other house." He was upset because he hadn't been there in a long time and he needed to go to work. Jennifer was worried Lee might try to run away and get there on his own.

She believed she knew the identity of the man whose life Lee was talking about. She was reluctant to give the name, be-cause the man had achieved some amount of fame and success, and the last thing she wanted anyone to think was that she was somehow looking for money.

We soon talked, and six weeks later, I flew out to the family's home to meet them. They live in a small Midwestern town of less than two thousand people that is fortunately only about twenty-five miles from a major airport. I sat down with Lee, his parents, and his fourteen-year-old sister. Jennifer's husband, William, a nonpracticing Catholic, was a truck driver, while Jennifer, a stay-at-home mother of three, including an eighteen-month-old, was somehow finding the time to return to college. She described herself as a nondenominational Christian and as "New Age." She reported a belief in reincarnation, but she felt this belief made her want to be extra cautious about Lee's statements. She had been careful not to ask him leading questions and not to automatically assume he was talking about a past life.

When Lee was about two and a half, he began mentioning his "other mommy." Initially, his parents didn't think much of it. Around that time, he insisted his middle name was Coe and said Coe was his mother's name as well. When his mother said her name was Jennifer, he said that was his daughter's name. For close to a year after that, he continued to insist his middle name was Coe whenever anyone mentioned his full name.

Lee then developed what Jennifer called an "obscene fascination" with Hollywood. He talked about it a lot and about his "other house." He said he had to go to Hollywood to go to work. William thought he might be talking about a past life. One day when Lee was three years and three months old, his family was sitting together and William asked Lee what he did in Hollywood. Lee said he worked on movies. William asked if he acted in movies, and Lee said no, he wrote movies.

Lee's parents began naming movies and asking if he had

written them. They report that when they got to the fifth or sixth one, *Gone with the Wind*, Lee said, "Yes, that was my movie. I wrote that movie." As Jennifer was looking up *Gone with the Wind* on the IMDb Web site, Lee's sister asked him how old he was when he died, and he said forty-eight. Jennifer then saw that the screenplay for *Gone with the Wind* was written by Sidney Coe Howard, who died when he was forty-eight. Lee's parents and his sister all remembered the conversation happening that way.

The idea that Lee had been Sidney Coe Howard in a past life explained other behaviors and statements he had made. As his third birthday was approaching in early June, Lee had insisted that his birthday was June 26, not June 21, which is his actual birthday. Children may want to celebrate their birthdays early, but few would insist their birthdays were later. Sidney Coe Howard was born on June 26, 1891. His mother's maiden name was Coe. His eldest child, his daughter from his first marriage, was named Jennifer.

One day, Jennifer, Lee's mother, asked him to tell her about Hollywood, but he refused. He said something that sounded like "Ohlawn." Jennifer asked what that was, and he said that was where his parents were. She asked him about his parents (whom he called his "other parents"), and he told a story about breaking a wheel on his mother's truck. He then started talking about Hollywood and said something about "Junai" (as Jennifer wrote, June eye? June nine?). When she couldn't figure out what he was trying to say, he got frustrated and stopped talking.

We never did figure out what "Junai" meant, but "Ohlawn" sounds pretty close to Oakland. Howard was born in Oakland, California, and his parents lived there until his father's death in 1915. His mother then moved to Berkeley, California, and eventually to New York City.

Lee would talk about his house in Hollywood and also said he had another house. He once told Jennifer that he had a tractor at his other house but that his people didn't take care of it. This seemed to refer to Howard's death, which was tragic. It happened on his farm in Massachusetts. He was planning to take his tractor, a Cleveland Cletrac crawler-type tractor that was a large piece of heavy machinery, out of the garage to work on a field he had recently purchased to extend his property. A hired hand had accidentally left the tractor in gear, and when Howard turned on the ignition switch and cranked it from the front, it lurched forward, pinning him against the stone foundation of the garage and crushing him.

Lee showed an aversion to anything tight around his upper body from the time he was a toddler. He hated being caught between Jennifer and a piece of furniture and even disliked being hugged tightly. He was also afraid of tractors. He was interested in them and thought they were cool, but he liked to keep his distance. When a neighbor got a new one, Lee didn't want to get close to it and wouldn't get on it even when it was turned off.

Lee also had nightmares, often on a nightly basis, that he usually couldn't describe. Jennifer e-mailed me the day after one of them. She had found him crying during the night, and when she asked him what was wrong, he said, "My arms are broken!" She said they were fine, but he insisted they were broken. When she asked him what happened, he said something that sounded like "cars on my arms." She asked, "A car is on your arms?" He said, "No, cars on my arms!" She asked again, and he yelled "No!" and then began waking up more.

At the end of my meeting with the family, I mentioned yet another television production. Thomas Breinholt, a Danish filmmaker, was working on a multipart series for Danish public television called *Soul and Science*. He interviewed me a week before my trip to see Lee's family. He asked if he could film me as I investigated a case, and I told him I would ask Lee's parents when I met them. When I brought it up with them, I explained that while the series would only be broadcast in Scandinavia, it was certainly possible clips could end up on YouTube or other sites. Lee's father said filming would be fine with him. I had the sense he didn't really care what people thought about him.

Jennifer was more hesitant. She was concerned about any effects that being on television talking about a past life might have on Lee down the line. She didn't mind the family's faces being shown, but she didn't want their names to appear on an Internet search. Afterward, Thomas Breinholt said he would be happy to withhold the family's full names and their location. Reassured, Jennifer agreed to be filmed, and we made plans for another interview. I would meet Thomas at the airport on a Monday morning, and we would go to the family's home for a noon meeting.

This meant I would leave Charlottesville on an early morning flight. Except that I then received a *very* early morning telephone call from the airline with an automated message that my flight had been canceled. When I was able to track down Thomas and tell him the news, he was understandably upset, since a major reason why he had flown over from Denmark was to film my interview with the family. That meant moving to Plan B, which was that Thomas would film the family talking about their experiences without me. Except that William's truck broke down in Missouri, so he wasn't there for the interview either. Even so, Thomas's meeting with the rest of the family went fine, and he seemed pleased with the footage he was able to get. At one point during the day, Lee's sister pulled up a clip of me on YouTube. Lee, who had just turned four, exclaimed, "Why is Dr. Tucker on the computer? He's supposed to be here!"

Thomas asked Jennifer about the possibility of taking Lee to places where Sidney Coe Howard had lived to see what his reactions would be, and she agreed. That meant we needed to do some research. Thomas was able to find some information online about places where Howard had lived and about his children. I then discovered that one of his daughters was living in the tiny Massachusetts village where Howard had died. It was fairly easy to find her address and phone number.

With some trepidation about bothering a seventy-seven-year-old woman with an admittedly unusual request, I wrote to her. I told her about Lee's statements and said I would love the opportunity to review all of them with her to find out how well they matched her father's life. I also wanted to take Lee to places that were meaningful to her father to observe any reactions he might have. I explained how I had found her, apologized for the intrusion, and said I hoped the letter was not disturbing to her and hoped to hear back from her soon.

A few days later, Howard's daughter called. She stated up front that she felt ninety percent skeptical about the situation, but she also seemed intrigued because, as she said, no one knew about her father anymore. She wrote afterward that she was reassured by our conversation. She also supplied personal information about her father that was not available online, such as pets he had as well as people who worked for him. I then sent Jennifer some topics to ask Lee about if she caught him in the mood to talk about Howard.

Howard's daughter was living on the farm where her father had died. She was open to letting us visit, and she mentioned that a summer theater her father had been very connected with was in nearby Stockbridge. I thought a trip to Massachusetts made more sense than taking Lee to Los Angeles. Howard had not actually owned a home in Hollywood, though he had rented particular places when he was there working. In addition, we would have full access to the Massachusetts house. One potential hitch was that Howard's daughter and her family always closed up the farmhouse in the fall and spent winters in New York City, where the weather was better. With it being September at the time, we had a fairly narrow window for a meeting.

We picked out a date, but as we were discussing arrangements, a new issue surfaced. Lee's father, William, was offered a job at the airport nearby. His training would end just before our planned trip, but he didn't know his work schedule after that. We planned a trip but William's schedule kept getting changed so much that we eventually had to cancel it. That was probably for the best because Howard's daughter e-mailed afterward to say a nor'easter hit the day we had planned to arrive, with fierce winds and lashing rains all day. She was open to a visit six months down the line, after cold weather and some renovations on the house were over.

In the intervening months, Lee became more reluctant to talk about Hollywood. Jennifer sensed he was embarrassed if her family asked him about it, as he thought they were making fun of him. Even so, he would often make minor comments to his mother about when he was big, things like, "When I was big, I had a blue shirt like this."

We were eventually able to make the trip to Massachusetts in the spring. At that point, Lee was about to turn five, and his talk about Hollywood had trailed off considerably. I met up with Lee and his parents at the airport, and we drove to the Howard farm on a pleasant Saturday morning. We met Howard's daughter along with her husband and her sister, Howard's youngest, who was only ten months old when he died. All three of them were wonderful—dignified but quite friendly. I don't know what they thought of the whole exercise, but they were respectful of the process and completely forthcoming.

We met at the house. Renovations to the kitchen were still ongoing, though they were largely done and looked beautiful. Howard's daughter showed us the interior of the home, pointing out changes that had been made over the years. Lee showed no reaction to meeting the family or seeing the house. We saw the grounds and then all spent some time talking by the pond. Howard's daughter also took us by nearby sites that Howard had frequented, including the place where he was killed, but again, Lee showed no response.

The family served us a picnic lunch on their large back porch. Afterward, I showed Lee some pictures of people from Howard's life. One was of Howard himself, but the others were pictures of people I thought Lee and his parents would not have stumbled across by accident, such as Howard's first wife, a couple of people he had worked with, and his father-in-law, a conductor named Walter Damrosch. Lee's parents could have helped him cram for the visit, but after meeting them, I didn't doubt their sincerity. Short of fraud, routine explanations would be difficult to come by if Lee recognized the people in the pictures. I didn't show him lineups as I had Ryan but rather just presented him one picture at a time to see if he recognized anyone. He did not.

All in all, the visit was uneventful. Perhaps if we had gotten there six months earlier, things would have been different, though of course we have no way of knowing. We do know that by the time of our trip, Lee was not talking about Hollywood as he had earlier.

If Lee's family is remembering his early comments correctly—that his middle name was Coe, that he wrote *Gone with the Wind*, had a daughter named Jennifer, and died when he was forty-eight—then he showed unusual knowledge about Sidney Howard's life. He talked about some smaller details as well, but Howard's daughter was not able to confirm them. For instance, Lee said he had a red tractor at his other house. Howard had a John Deere that was presumably green, but his daughter did not know the color of the Cleveland Cletrac that killed him. I looked online and found pictures of models made at the time Howard died that were indeed red, but there is no record of the color of his particular tractor. Howard's daughter did say she felt sure his mother had never owned a truck, as Lee had described, but that perhaps there was one that belonged to a gardener.

Since Lee did not give any personal information that could be verified to match Howard's life but that was not readily available online, his case does not provide the level of evidence of a past-life connection that James's and Ryan's do. Even so, in considering his statements as well as his behaviors, I can't dismiss it either. The case as a whole remains somewhat unresolved but intriguing nonetheless.

A GOLF CHANNEL

This next case is most notable for the child's behavior and abilities. I first heard from his father when the boy was three. He reported that his son Hunter had received a set of plastic golf clubs when he turned two. He loved the clubs and played with them incessantly. A few months later, Hunter's father was running through the television channels when he passed the Golf Channel. Neither of Hunter's parents played golf, and his father hadn't even known the family got the Golf Channel. Once Hunter saw it, he told his parents to go back to it. From then on, he had no interest in children's shows and wanted to watch nothing but the Golf Channel. His parents had to limit him to thirty minutes in the morning and again at night.

One day, there was an infomercial about Bobby Jones, a famous golfer in the 1920s whose name is now used by a company that makes golf equipment and accessories. When Hunter saw the program, he told his parents he had been Bobby Jones when he was big. He said this repeatedly, and when someone would ask him what his name was, he would say Bobby Jones. He wanted to be called Bobby and would correct people if they called him Hunter. He would also correct them if they called him Tiger or any other name. He knew of Tiger Woods and other golfers from the Golf Channel, and though he liked them, he was much more passionate about Bobby Jones.

His parents initially laughed about all this. They were both raised Christian. His father had read some about Buddhism, however, and was intrigued by the idea of rebirth. He decided to test Hunter. He showed Hunter pictures of six golfers from the 1920s and asked him which one was Bobby Jones. Hunter pointed at the picture of Bobby Jones and said, "This me." That might not be so surprising, but he then pointed to the picture of another golfer, Harry Vardon. Hunter said, "This, Harry Garden. My friend." Hunter's father printed pictures off the Internet of several houses, including Bobby Jones's childhood home. When he showed them to Hunter, he said, "House, house, house" as he pointed to each picture until he got to

Bobby Jones's home. He suddenly appeared wistful as he said, "Home." His dad thought Hunter had not seen either Harry Vardon or Bobby Jones's childhood home before, and was shocked.

Hunter would take his little golf clubs wherever he went. When he practiced at the beach, he would call it the sand trap. Golfers would see him practicing and comment on what a great swing he had. His parents gave him a set of real golf clubs for Christmas, and he then began taking lessons at a golf club. The usual starting age for lessons was five, but when the staff saw Hunter's swing, they accepted him while he was still two. His instructor called him a golf prodigy. Several older golfers commented that Hunter's swing reminded them of Bobby Jones. Not being a golfer, I'm not in a position to judge any resemblance, but he seemed to show a similar front leg move.

When Hunter was three, his mother was putting him to bed one night as they talked about him being his parents' child. He said, "Just like my child?" When his mother asked him his child's name, Hunter answered, "Bobby Jones. He was my son." Bobby Jones did indeed have a son named after him, Robert Tyre Jones III, and I later found a mention from a *Time* magazine article that referred to the son as "young Bobby" when he was fourteen.

When I got the report from Hunter's father, I quickly asked about visiting the family. His parents were agreeable to a meeting, and we soon worked out a time for me to visit them at their home in sunny Southern California. Hunter's parents were very pleasant and cooperative, and Hunter, a few months past his third birthday, was very cute. I brought along some pictures of Bobby Jones with other golfers, but I wasn't able to get Hunter engaged enough in looking at them to give me any feedback.

We finished out in the yard as I watched Hunter hitting golf balls into a net. Even if the visit didn't produce new information, it was useful in that it gave me the chance to review the history with Hunter's parents and to see that they came across as reasonable, responsible people.

I received an update from Hunter's father a year later. Hunter had said very little in the interim about Bobby Jones or any memories, but he remained obsessed with golf. Not only did he enjoy playing it, he would also spend time at night designing golf courses with his blankets, which he would then show to his parents. His favorite real course was Augusta National, home of the Masters Tournament. Bobby Jones founded the Augusta National Golf Club and helped design the course.

When Hunter was three and a half, a friend of the president of the local GolfTEC, an outfit with numerous centers around the country, saw Hunter playing golf and was impressed. He connected the family to GolfTEC, which let Hunter begin weekly lessons with a PGA Golf pro. They called him a prodigy there and said he had a natural swing. His father emphasized to me that he and his wife weren't pushing Hunter to play golf. They had him in a soccer league, and he enjoyed various activities. But he continued to ask to go to the driving range and to golf courses.

After another year passed, Hunter's father sent me a video of Hunter playing golf. Although I'm not a golfer, even I could tell he was exceptional. It was hard to believe that this smooth swing was coming from a five-year-old.

Hunter is now seven. At last count, he had won forty-one out of fifty junior golf tournaments, including twenty-one in a row. During the week his father wrote me with an update, Hunter had just competed in the six- to-nine-year-old division of a local tournament and won it by ten strokes. He was doing well in other areas, too. As he was completing the first grade, he was reading, writing, and doing math at a third grade level.

Hunter's obsession with golf is reminiscent of James Leininger's obsession with planes. Such behavior is common in our cases. Many of the children show themes in their play that appear connected to the past-life memories they report, most often related to the occupation of the previous person. That doesn't often allow them to show special skill at the occupation; for instance, a toddler like James could hardly show proficiency in flying a plane. In Hunter's case, golf is an area that has allowed him to show exceptional ability.

In nine percent of our cases, the children are said to have unusual skills related to the previous life. This often involves the family's subjective opinion that their child was able to perform an activity better than children would normally be expected to. In Hunter's case, winning twenty-one golf tournaments in a row is more than a subjective opinion. He clearly has unusual ability in golf.

Some people have wondered if the talents that prodigies show come from previous lives. We certainly have little understanding about where they do come from. How does a Mozart come along, composing by age five and performing exhibitions by age six? In his case, his father was a music teacher, but there have presumably been countless music teacher parents who tried to groom their children but didn't produce Mozarts.

I've always resisted ascribing a past life to prodigies, because unless they talk about prior memories, I wouldn't make the leap that this poorly understood phenomenon is due to past lives. Ian likewise never made that claim. When he wrote a paper on abnormalities that are not fully explicable by genetics and/or environmental influences, he did discuss precociously expressed interests and goals that some children have had without an obvious stimulus. His examples included Georg Friedrich Händel the composer and Florence Nightingale, the founder of modern nursing. He noted that as far as he knew, none of the people he listed ever remembered having a previous life, but he argued that the early intensity of their striving toward unusual goals had no explanation in their genetics or early environments. He also pointed out that the children we've studied have sometimes shown unusual aptitudes, but not fully formed skills that geniuses like Mozart manifested as children.

Hunter may be an exception. I suppose the difference between unusual aptitudes and fully formed skills can be in the eye of the beholder, but to say that Hunter showed an unusual aptitude for golf at a young age seems to be an understatement. He has received coaching early on, but only because of the skill he showed before that. While he hasn't accomplished anything comparable to what Mozart did as a child, he seems to be, if not a prodigy, one really good golfer at an early age. And his skills correspond to his very early claims about a past life.

Lee and Hunter both claimed to be well-known figures. Though Sidney Coe Howard is no longer remembered by the general public, Bobby Jones remains a familiar name to many people. That may cause you to doubt Hunter's statements. Both of these cases, however, show little in common with the case of Kenedi, the boy in Turkey. Kenedi's father admired John Kennedy greatly, whereas Hunter's parents had little interest in golf and Lee's parents had never heard of Sidney Coe Howard. Despite my own hesitancy about cases involving well-known figures, I think these two demonstrate that some of them should be taken seriously.

Along with the well-known figures, another characteristic these cases share is that both of the children reporting the memories were boys. This is not surprising, as sixty-two percent of our subjects are male. We have wondered why more boys than girls talk about past lives. Since ninety percent of the children talk about a life as a member of the same sex, another way of considering the question is to ask why more of the past lives involve males. Ian speculated that women's lives on the whole might not have as much variety and excitement—and thus be as memorable—as men's lives in the cultures where he studied cases (he was specifically referring to cases in Burma). This would lead to fewer female lives being remembered. That's a reasonable possibility but not, it turns out, the correct explanation. We no longer have to speculate because now that we have two thousand cases coded and entered into our database, I think we have a definite answer.

In cases in which the cause of death is known, only thirty percent of the previous individuals died by natural causes. Those cases include roughly fifty percent males and fifty percent females, there being slightly more male deaths than female ones (which seems to also be true in the general population).

The other seventy percent of our cases involve unnatural deaths, including murders, suicides, and accidental deaths. (I'll discuss the issue of unnatural deaths more in an upcoming chapter.) It's in those cases where the difference in the sexes shows up. Seventy-three percent of the time, the cases involved males.

Unnatural deaths in the general population show the same pattern. Men are more likely to die an unnatural death than women because they engage more in high-risk behaviors such as driving too fast, getting into drunken knife fights, and so forth. I found statistics for five years of deaths in the United States and checked the male-to-female ratio. I discovered that males accounted for seventy-two percent of the unnatural deaths.

I was quite impressed by how the male/female percentages in our cases match up with those in the general population. If the children are fantasizing about past lives I can think of no reason why this would be the case, why the types of death broken down by gender would have the exact same percentages as the general population. On the other hand, if the children really are recalling past lives, you would expect a random sample of two thousand to have the same percentage of males and females as the total population. We have more males overall because so many of our cases involve unnatural deaths. But within the categories of causes of death, the ratio of males to females matches perfectly with the general population, which I take as further evidence that the children's memories may well be valid.

Chapter 7

IDENTITY UNKNOWN

In our strongest cases, a deceased individual has been found whose life matches the details the child has given. In that situation, we say it is a solved case. We also have a number in which no one has identified one particular person from the past whose life the child appears to be remembering. Those we call unsolved, and they make up almost thirty percent of our collection. With the unsolved ones, we have to consider more the possibility that the children are either experiencing a fantasy or even making up stories intentionally. But I don't think we should dismiss these cases out of hand. Some can be quite compelling. At the very least, they raise the question of what could possibly lead young children to believe they remember the events some of these children report.

A TRAUMATIC WALK DOWN A DUSTY ROAD

I met a woman at a conference a while back who has had a memory of another life since she was a child. Susan, an accomplished clinical psychologist, has told no one about this except her husband. He was accepting, feeling that reincarnation is as likely as anything else, but they take their children to a Protestant church. She does not remember if she even told her mother about the memory, but she knows she told no one else.

Beginning at a very early age, Susan, who is Caucasian, remembers being an African American girl of seven or eight walking down a dirt road. Susan grew up in a mountainous area, but the environment in her memory is different. It is hot, humid, flat, and very dusty; Susan thinks it is probably in the Southeast United States. As she is walking, she looks down at the dry skin of her hands and thinks they look "ashy."

A car comes up, one perhaps from the 1940s, and she is suddenly yanked into it. There are two white men in the car, grown men in their twenties or thirties, the driver and the one who pulled her in. She remembers the bench seat, the lines of the upholstery, the dusty floorboard. There, in the car, she is raped and murdered.

Susan's recall of this was as much a memory for her as anything from her childhood. She also had repetitive dreams about the event. In some of them, she re-experienced it. In others, she observed what happened from above. She didn't think of the dreams as nightmares, but they did wake her up frequently.

Susan also had, and still has, an exaggerated startle response, meaning that a little noise that surprises her can make her jump much more than most people. She doesn't remember being excessively anxious about her safety as a child, but she did worry a lot about her father. He was a surgeon who worked long hours, and Susan would irritate her mother when she delayed dinner by insisting on watching for his car to come down the road, which meant that he was safe. Her mother took her to a counselor at one point for psychotherapy. Susan was quite young and does not remember anything about the treatment. She thinks that perhaps she had told her mother about her memory, leading her mother to take her to the therapist.

Susan knows of no stimulus in her environment that would have caused her to have such a memory. There were African Americans living in her town but no particular racial unrest. It was only later when she was cheerleading that a black friend on the squad told her that when African Americans' skin gets so dry that it looks gray, they call it "ashy."

Susan attended a Methodist church growing up, where she presumably was not taught about past-life memories. Her mother was raised Catholic, though she was open to various ideas about religion. Susan definitely did not learn about past lives from her father. The son of a minister, he said he had gotten his fill of church as a child, and he was resolutely a man of logic and science. When Susan asked him why we are here, he said to reproduce. When she asked what happens when we die, he explained how the body decomposes.

Susan took a philosophy class in high school and did a project on Emanuel Swedenborg, the scientist turned mystic. Though Swedenborg did not believe in reincarnation, his ideas about how people create their afterlife by the way they live their lives here were ones she found quite meaningful. Her subsequent work as a psychologist, however, has been more behaviorally based and completely mainstream. She feels her memories had no negative effects on her as she grew older, causing no impact on her sexual relationships and no ongoing anxiety problems other than the continuation of her exaggerated startle response.

Susan has also experienced migraines all her life. Even though people have told her it's impossible, she remembers seeing the visual phenomena that can precede migraines—flashing lines of light—through the slats of her crib. She has thus maintained some very early memories. Along with those, she has apparently maintained some memories of a past life as well, not some happy fantasy to be sure but rather the mundane details of a horrific event.

Erlendur Haraldsson, a colleague, has suggested that some of these children might be experiencing posttraumatic stress disorder (PTSD). Many do have persistent images of a violent death, and some groups of children Erlendur has studied in Asia showed more symptoms of anxiety and aggression than samples of children without past-life memories. The symptoms, however, were mild, and many of the individual children did not show them.

In general, though I wouldn't say that most of the children have PTSD, many do talk repeatedly about a traumatic memory. Also, in the cases in which the previous person died an unnatural death, over thirty-five percent of the children show an intense fear of the mode of death, the kind of avoidant behavior that is part of the official DSM criteria for PTSD. Susan showed some post-traumatic symptoms. Along with her persistent daytime memories, she had repeated dreams about the traumatic event. She also had some anxiety and an exaggerated startle response, another criterion for PTSD. She may not have had enough difficulties to warrant the full diagnosis, but she did show symptoms of it, just as James Leininger showed post-traumatic symptoms related to a plane crash. There seemed to be no reason for Susan to develop a fantasy that she was raped and murdered as an African American girl in another part of the country, and certainly no reason for her to develop post-traumatic symptoms from it. If the images she experienced were what they seem to be, it was not a fantasy that traumatized her; it was a memory.

In the following two groups of cases, I've corresponded with the parents or subjects but not met them face to face. Though the children involved haven't given details that could lead to a successful search for a previous person, each case has notable facets. The cases serve as examples of what numerous families are experiencing, as we get these kinds of reports all the time. I could choose many other similar ones to present, but these are some that have recently caught my attention.

THE THINGS LITTLE GIRLS SAY

A father from Canada e-mailed me about his daughter. He explained that during his own childhood, he never had any interest in hockey. This was a great source of disappointment to his father, who was quite passionate about it and wanted to share that passion with his son. Because of the difference, the son never felt his father's love, and they never became close.

As an adult, this man not only disliked hockey but resented it, because of the difficulties it had caused him. When he met his future wife, he told her they would get along fine as long as she never talked to him about hockey or wanted to watch a hockey game on television.

They had a daughter named Hannah. They tended to be overprotective parents, and since their work schedules were different—the wife working days while her husband had his own business and worked nights—they never used a sitter until Hannah was nine years old, when her grandmother began to watch her.

Like her parents, Hannah had never expressed any interest

in hockey before a conversation when she was three years old. She asked her father that day why her son didn't come around to take her to hockey games anymore. He asked her when her son had done this, and she said, "You know, Daddy, when I was an old lady." For a couple of months, she asked about her son and seemed frustrated that he wasn't coming around.

Hannah gave details about her son. She said he was skinny and had curly, red hair. Though Hannah's parents were vegetarian and didn't wear leather, she talked about how her son wore a leather coat that, based on where she pointed on her father as she told him about it, was a three-quarter length coat. She said he drove a white car that had some rust on it. She also used the word *arena*, which her father found remarkable, as Hannah had never been to an arena and he thought no one would have had a reason to talk about one around her.

Hannah then stopped talking about her son and hockey games. When her father asked her about those things a few months later, she seemed to have no memory of them.

Even though the child's statements can't be verified in this case, I find it quite striking. What would possess a three-year-old, especially one whose family didn't even like hockey, to imagine she had been an elderly woman wanting her son to take her to hockey games?

The same month that I first heard from Hannah's dad, I received a letter from a father in the Midwest. He reported that when his daughter Chelsea was around three years old, she talked about a friend named Dorn, telling her mother first and a day or two later her father. She said that she and Dorn were playing in a muddy street when some bad men rode up on horses and killed her friend. Some policemen in round hats showed up later to talk about it.

This story was quite unlike the things she normally talked about, in the level of detail as well as the subject matter. Her father noted that the images certainly didn't match any events she had experienced and that she was never left unattended to watch television on her own. When he asked her a question about it a few weeks later, she answered in a way that made him think the memories were in her mind to stay. When he brought it up again after a much longer interval, however, she seemed to have no idea what he was talking about.

Chelsea is a young adult now. Her father says she has no recollection of her story about Dorn and thinks it sounds a bit odd. Though it may, it fits the patterns we see in a lot of our cases. While most of the children describe suffering a traumatic death themselves, some talk of witnessing violence or experiencing nonfatal trauma. Her age fits the typical case, and like most of our subjects, she seemed to forget all about her previous report as she got older.

The next case has a couple of strengths. Not only did the girl's mother keep notes of her statements, she also performed a test that the girl passed.

Olivia is a British girl whose family has lived in various parts of the world. Her mother was raised Catholic but was uninterested in religion as an adult, describing herself as an "agnostic atheist." Olivia seemed to talk about two past lives, but I want to focus on one of them. When Olivia was two years old, she and her mother were out walking when her mother asked Olivia what time she thought it was. Olivia said, "seven o'clock" then added, "1789." Her mother repeated, "1789?" Olivia thought for a minute and said with conviction, "No, 1787."

The following month, Olivia and her parents were riding on a bus when her mother commented that Olivia's furry white hat with ears made her look like a lamb. Olivia began talking about taking all the "fur off a lamb." She said that after taking off the fur, you brush all the dust out of the hair. She added that this was very important.

While still two years old, Olivia came to her mother one day and told her quite matter-of-factly that her name used to be Daisy. Some time later, she approached her mother again and out of the blue said, "Robinson." Her mother asked what that meant, and Olivia said, "It's a name." Her mother asked her whose name, and Olivia replied, "It was *my* name." She told her mother that she used to be Daisy Robinson.

Olivia talked about past events a number of times when she was two and a half. Her father began to wonder if she was remembering a past life, but when he would ask her, "Have you got another mummy and daddy?" she always looked puzzled and said no. When he asked her one time if she *used to* have a different mummy and daddy, she became excited and said yes. Her parents asked about any brothers or sisters, and she said she didn't have any. They mentioned the sheep shearing and asked what she used to make. She answered, "blankets," which her mother found striking since Olivia had seen sheep skin rugs before but never a woolen blanket.

Olivia came up to her mother one day as she was doing housework. Olivia told her, "All the air came out of here." Her mother didn't know what she was talking about and asked, "Out of where?" Olivia pointed to the middle of her body and said, "Here. And I died. But I don't like talking about it." She looked sad and turned around and left the room. Her mother was stunned by this. Olivia had had no contact with death, other than seeing a dead frog once that her parents hadn't even told her was dead.

One day after waking up from a nap, Olivia was sitting up

on her cot and began telling her mother again about 1787. Her mother asked if she had known any songs back then, and Olivia immediately said, "London Bridge Is Falling Down," which was a favorite of hers. It turns out that "London Bridge Is Falling Down" was in fact around in 1787. The words of an early version appeared in *Tommy Thumb's Pretty Song Book* around 1744, and it may well be much older than that. The dance "London Bridge" was mentioned in a 1659 play, and "London Bridge Is Broken Down" was associated with children in a 1725 publication and mentioned in a London opera in 1730.

Another time, Olivia approached her mother and out of the blue said, "Thirty years old." When her mother asked who was thirty years old, she said, "I was. When I died. I died because I didn't eat anything." She then wandered away. After her mother got over the shock of what her two-and-a-half-year-old had just said, she began thinking that the voracious appetite Olivia had shown from the time she was a newborn could be explained by starvation she had experienced in a previous life.

Olivia was eating a green apple one day when she began giggling to herself. She told her mother that Daisy Robinson had only eaten red apples but that she only liked green apples now. This seemed funny to her. Another time, she said that Daisy Robinson's mother had been named Kitty. Olivia didn't know anyone named Kitty, and her mother felt sure she had never heard the name used for a person before.

Olivia's talk about past lives then stopped for a long time. Her mother thought she had forgotten about them until a conversation after the family's dog died. Olivia was four at that point, and her comments were interesting enough that her mother grabbed a pen and paper and made notes as she talked. Olivia wondered if the dog would come back as another dog and said she thought it would because she had had past lives herself. But she didn't think their dog was a new doggy yet because, she said, "you spend a bit of time dead first, like a few weeks or a few months or something."

Her mom asked if that happened to her, and Olivia said yes. When her mother asked where she was after she died, she said she didn't exist. She said that it was hard to explain but that she went into thin air. She went up into the sky and broke up into bits of dust. The dust then floated all over the place. She said dying wasn't scary, and when she was dust, other people made friends with her. They were dust as well. Her mother asked if she was scared of dying now. Olivia said no, she wasn't scared, but the thought of dying did make her sad because she liked being on Earth. Olivia was extremely serious throughout the conversation. In fact, her mother said Olivia had such a serious look in her eyes that it made her uncomfortable.

Olivia then seemed to move on, and her mother didn't hear about past lives again until one day when Olivia was five years and nine months old. Olivia began a conversation by asking her mother if it was silly to believe in something if there isn't any proof. They discussed that question, with her mom using the belief in God as an example of something that some people can't believe without proof while others do so easily.

Olivia then said that when she was Daisy, she believed in God and she went to church. Her mother wondered why she used to believe in God but didn't now. Olivia said that was because she was a different person now. Her mother told her she thought that Olivia might have the same personality that Daisy had, but Olivia said no, the personality was gone but the person was still there. Her mom asked if she meant that a "person" and a "personality" are two different things, and Olivia said yes.

As they talked about Daisy's life, Olivia said she lived in a little town. She didn't remember the name of it but did remember it was in England. She said most people lived in little villages where everybody knew each other. She said there were a few shops, and you could buy bread, cheese, and meat. Her mother, with a straight face, asked her if there was a McDonald's in the town. Olivia laughed and said it wasn't invented yet. She said they didn't even have cars, only horses. Olivia then said she remembered the money they used had the king on it. She said the coins were bumpy on the edges and very flat.

Olivia's mother investigated English coins from 1787, the year Olivia had previously given for Daisy. They all had the picture of King George III on them. They had serrated edges and were flatter than the modern-day £2 coin. She decided to show Olivia pictures of various coins, fifty-two in all, that ranged from ancient Celtic and Roman coins all the way to modern-day ones. She asked Olivia if any of them were familiar to her. Olivia looked through them all, quickly dismissing ancient hammered ones as well as modern-day coins. When she saw a page of milled coins, machine-made as all English coins have been since the 1600s, she pointed to the dots around the edges of one of them and said that was what she meant when she said the coins were bumpy.

Olivia then pointed to a 1787 George III shilling and said she definitely recognized the coin and the picture of the king on it. She pointed to three other coins she said she remembered. All of them were George III coins: a spade guinea from 1793, a Somerset Bristol halfpenny token from 1793, and a farthing from 1799 that she said was vaguely familiar.

Olivia's mother once told her she thought her past lives must be some kind of game she was playing. Olivia became upset and vehemently denied it. When her mother saw her engaging in role-play make-believe another time, she asked Olivia if it was only a game, and Olivia said yes. Her mother noted how different the two activities were: how she could identify elements from a favorite movie or book or play in the role-play but not in the past-life talk; how the details changed frequently, sometimes in seconds, in the role-play but never in the past-life talk, even over months and years. She knew Olivia believed her memories were real, and after a while, she struggled to find any reason to doubt her.

IN DREAMS

I tend to be leery of claims that someone's dreams are events from a past life. Dreams are complex things, often puzzling and frequently nonsensical. Some of the cases I've described have included dreams, of course, but they also involved waking statements as well. If a case only involves dreams, I don't tend to make too much of it. Occasionally, however, we get reports that impress me.

One came from a man who reported that he had the same dream over and over from age three to around age seven. It involved being a little boy playing at the seashore where there were crowds of people. In the dream, the ocean began to recede, and as it did, he could see fish flopping on the wet sand where the ocean had been moments before. He and others began wandering out onto the wet sand, amazed that the ocean had pulled back for what appeared to be miles.

He continued to walk farther and farther out, picking up giant shells, some of which still had living creatures wiggling inside. He then began hearing screams, lots of screams, coming from men, women, and children who were running back toward the beach. He looked up and saw the ocean, which was still far away but now appeared as a giant wall of water. It was rushing forward as people frantically tried to escape it. He remembered seeing it over his shoulder as it got closer and closer until it finally loomed over him and crashed down on him. He would drown in the dream and then wake up in his bed.

For a long time, the man didn't make much of the dream. His family often went to the beach when he was growing up, and though the dreams were terrifying, he had no fear of the ocean. When he was around the age of twenty-five, he was shocked to learn that the ocean really can recede, as it does before a tsunami. It was only then, as he wondered how he could have possibly known about a receding ocean as a three-year-old in the early 1950s, that he began to view the events he experienced not only as a dream but also as memories from a previous life.

Another man recently emailed me with similar dream experiences. Like the previous one, he repeatedly had the dream when he was a little boy, dreaming the identical scene dozens of times until he was five or six years old. It was always exactly the same, and he reported that even now in his fifties, he can still remember the details vividly.

In the dream, he appears to be storming the beach with a group of soldiers or warriors. They are in waist-deep water moving toward the shore, where there is a large stone wall or fortress. People are on top of the wall shooting arrows at the incoming force. He remembers seeing the arrows moving like dark sticks against the light blue sky. One is then speeding toward him and hits him in the chest. It knocks him backward, and the next thing he remembers is being dragged onto the beach by two other men. He can see the end of the arrow sticking out of his chest as one of the men attempts to pull it out. There is chaos around him as he slowly fades away. He remembers seeing the blue sky with small, white clouds, until his vision closes in and the world goes dark.

The man had sensed as a child that he was big in the dream. He feels he was bigger then than he is now as an adult. He also reports that even though the dream was entirely from a first-person point of view, he can picture the face of the man in it, one with long, reddish hair and a beard. The image reminds him of a Viking warrior, and he is convinced that he remembered his death from a previous life.

A FIRE ON C STREET

With this last case, I did meet the girl and her parents. Even though I wasn't able to verify that she was remembering the life of a particular individual, some of the things she said and did were definitely out of the ordinary.

My first contact with the family was an e-mail from the girl's mother, Kathleen. At the time, Nicole was twenty-two months old. Her first unusual behavior had been at thirteen months of age when her parents placed her on a horse. She grabbed the saddle horn with her left hand and the reins with her right, sat upright, and began kicking. Her parents didn't own horses and knew little about them. At seventeen months of age, Nicole began making the clicking sound in her throat that riders often do to get their horses to walk. At twenty-two months, she verbalized a series of equestrian commands that she could not have learned from her parents.

Kathleen, while confessing she was hesitant to mention it since I was a psychiatrist, also noted that Nicole often had conversations with people who weren't there. After I wrote back and assured her that I didn't think such behavior in a twenty-two-month-old indicated a psychiatric disturbance, she shared more.

Kathleen's brother Mike had died about six months before. For the last twenty-five years of his life, he had been wheelchair bound after being hit by a train and losing his legs. Kathleen, the only person to ever call him Mikey, saw him very little during the twenty years before his death.

Nicole has two mothers, Kathleen and her partner Lynn. A few weeks before Kathleen first contacted me, Nicole was at the breakfast table one morning when Lynn noticed her staring outside. Lynn asked her what she saw, and Nicole began yelling something Lynn couldn't make out. Lynn said she didn't understand and asked again what Nicole saw. Nicole started yelling, "Mikey, Mikey, Mikey!" Lynn asked if Nicole saw Uncle Mikey and asked where he was. Nicole yelled, "Right dere, outside." Lynn could see that no one was outside and asked again where Mikey was. Nicole responded, "Right dere, in chair."

A couple of weeks later, Nicole was recounting her day's events with her parents, and she again talked about seeing Mikey outside in his chair. This unnerved her parents, and Kathleen wrote to me a few days later. She said she and Lynn wanted to be careful not to lead Nicole to make up things while at the same time encouraging her to feel safe sharing any experiences she was having.

Nicole mentioned Mike several more times, saying he was in a chair. She had never met him, so Kathleen showed her a few photographs of him. Nicole showed no signs at all of recognizing him. If she was seeing visions of him, he looked different in some way than he did in the pictures.

I didn't hear from Kathleen for a while, until soon after Nicole's third birthday. She reported that Nicole had stopped talking about Mike. When Kathleen had asked her a few months before if she saw Mike anymore, she said no, but that she still remembered him. Kathleen asked what she remembered, and she said solemnly, "I remember the train." Kathleen had never talked to Nicole about the accident, and when she asked what she remembered about the train, Nicole said the sound of the wheels on the track. Kathleen was struck by this because Mike had described that sound as one of his last recollections before being hit. He said he was haunted by it. Kathleen noted that Nicole had never liked trains from infancy on. When she was a year or so old, her parents had to remove her from a room after she began wailing at the sounds that a model train was making.

While Nicole's talk about Mike receded, she began talking more about a time when she lived on C Street (or perhaps, Sea or even Seay Street). Her first comments began before she was two years old and then increased over time. She said the house on C Street was in an area that was sunny, not like the Pacific Northwest where her family lived. She said she lived there with her father, her sisters, and her best friend, a man. She had been the middle of three sisters, with the youngest being named Jackie. At one point, she described her father dancing in a suit at a wedding. She also said her father cut the branches off of trees and cut down the big old trees and made them float in the water. She talked repeatedly about the house on C Street burning down. Kathleen noted that Nicole seemed to go back and forth between memories and make-believe, but both Kathleen and Lynn could tell a difference when she would switch to make-believe. Her voice would change, and she would begin to give fanciful names for people, like Kuka and Lala and Hoopty.

I asked Kathleen if the family would be open to a visit from me to learn more about what Nicole was saying. She and Lynn considered it for a while and then agreed. They asked

Nicole if she wanted to speak to me. She said, "Yes, but I will be a little shy of him." They told her she didn't have to talk to me if she didn't want to, and she then became emphatic, saying, "No, no, I want to talk to him. I will *not* be shy!" And she was right. Kathleen was concerned Nicole might become oppositional and not talk to me, but she needn't have worried. Nicole proved to be quite engaging, though she didn't share any new information about C Street with me.

I met the three of them in their home. At that point, Nicole was thirty-nine months old. Her parents talked about how she would often say she just wanted to go home. They would tell her she was home, and she would say, "Oh yeah, I am home." At times, she would appear very sad talking about people from C Street and had recently asked if her parents could take her to her "little house on C Street." She said the top of it was kind of orange and that it was right down the street from a church.

Nicole would talk about these things at various times, sometimes after waking up from a nap. She had also dreamed about something happening to her sisters from C Street. She spoke a lot about the fire there. She said she didn't die in it. She would make the sound of a fire and said how the backyard was all that was left afterward.

She once said that when she was twenty-eight, she had gotten covered in dirt and got in the water. She then rowed her dinghy across the water and landed in some trees but didn't get hurt (or "didn't have any owies" as she put it). Kathleen asked if she had said "thingy," and Nicole answered, "No, Momma, dinghy! It's a little boat!"

We had a very pleasant visit. The next day, the family was riding in their car when Nicole said she couldn't find her picture book. Kathleen asked what picture book, and Nicole said her picture album. Kathleen said the picture album she had made for Nicole was in her room, but Nicole said no, the picture album from her house on C Street, it got all burned up in the fire. She talked about a burnt picture album with the edges curled.

The impression that emerged was that Nicole seemed to be describing a life in which she had experienced a traumatic fire, probably when she was a child. She had survived the fire and lived to be an adult. In fact, she had talked of being a doctor.

If Nicole was remembering a past life, the big question was where C Street was. An online search reveals numerous towns with C Streets or Sea Streets or Seay Streets. In particular, it shows that C Street in Virginia City, Nevada, was destroyed along with most of the town in a large fire in 1875. I found an account of the fire that listed the buildings destroyed on C Street. Though they appear to have been primarily commercial, there were several lodging houses lost, and the list concludes with "and many other buildings."

Kathleen contacted a historian to learn more about the town. She asked about timber work and bodies of water, since Nicole had mentioned those. The answers were inconclusive. The historian reported that the hills there had been covered with ponderosa pine and cedar at one point, but all of it was clear cut. Wood was brought from Tahoe to run a gold mill, brought partially by flume, man-made canals that logs were floated down. There are lakes nearby, but no significant ones in the immediate area.

Virginia City was certainly a possibility. The problem was that we didn't know if Nicole was describing a great conflagration like the one there or a simple house fire. For instance, I found a news story about a wildfire that destroyed one house on C Street in Martinez, California, in 2004. Since there might have been numerous other fires of this sort, I decided that rather than taking Nicole to Virginia City to see if she recognized any buildings still there from the 1800s, I would wait to see if she came out with more information identifying a specific town. But she never did.

I heard from Kathleen intermittently over the next few months. As Nicole was nearing her fourth birthday, she said one day that remembering her C Street family took a lot out of her. A week or so later, she appeared sad, almost despondent, and said, "Maybe I never had a C Street family. Maybe I just made them all up." Her C Street family may have been her imagination—there is no way of knowing with certainty since I wasn't able to find a family that matched her statements—but she may also have been voicing confusion because her memories didn't fit with her increasing awareness of how life appears to go. She had begun to feel perhaps that since she couldn't have had a family previously, what she thought she remembered must not have happened. Kathleen and Lynn were sad that with Nicole's memories fading, she seemed to be disconnecting from the spiritual realm she had access to before.

The disconnection, however, was not complete, as Nicole occasionally talked about C Street for sometime. When she was five, she rarely mentioned it, but if her parents asked if it was real, she would emphatically respond, "Is real! C Street is still there!" She maintained that there was a fire but that she didn't die in it, and she would mention images from time to time, most often involving her father, the church nearby, and incidents with water and logging. She also gave little snippets about her life after the fire.

When Nicole was five and a half, the family visited a small gallery in another town. Nicole noticed a handcrafted black box with a Victrola speaker horn on top. She stopped suddenly and said, "Oh my gosh, I haven't seen one of these in years!" Kathleen asked if she knew what it was, and Nicole said, "Yes, Momma, it's a record player." Kathleen asked where she might have seen one, and Nicole answered, "C Street. We had one in the '30s." For the next twenty minutes, she was humming songs that she said she recalled hearing on her record player. Her parents were impressed by how pretty the tunes were, as well as by the sophistication of Nicole's humming. Several times, her voice got a tremolo, a trembling effect, in it. A couple of days later, Nicole said she used to go to sleep listening to music on that old record player.

Though I'm not sure of Nicole's timing when she said she had a record player like that in the '30s, as I gather phonographs with horn speakers were passé by then, the incident as a whole is impressive. Nicole's startled recognition upon seeing the phonograph, followed by her becoming engrossed in music she felt was from long ago, suggests to me that she was connecting with some kind of memory.

A month later, she talked about getting from C Street to her current life. She said she was just walking on C Street and then was in another world, where there was something blocking her and she couldn't get through. She was then suddenly in her mother's tummy. Nicole said, "I was like, 'This is weird, I'm little and I'm going to get born again. I'm a baby. This is so weird.'" She talked about feeling very small in the womb, and how it was dark and odd there.

When Nicole was six, she told Kathleen, "Mom, you know when I came out of your tummy, this life turned out to be way more fun and laughter than I was expecting."

When Nicole was seven, she was getting in the car to go to school one day when she stopped, closed her eyes, and tilted her head back. "I feel there's an earthquake coming," she said. She said it wouldn't be in her state (in the Pacific Northwest) but very close. Kathleen told some colleagues at work about it. That evening, Nicole was puzzled that there hadn't been an earthquake. The next day, one of Kathleen's co-workers came running up and asked if she had heard about the 6.0 earthquake that hit off the Oregon coast the night before.

Such incidents suggest that Nicole, like Ryan in chapter 5, has some psychic abilities, again raising the question of where her past-life images came from. Were they actual memories, or were they material Nicole saw psychically? And more important, could psychic abilities explain all apparent past-life memories? Since I reviewed this issue in my first book, I won't go through the whole discussion again, except to point out that most of the children in our cases do not show any psychic abilities. At last count, only twenty-six percent of the families have said the children displayed any ESP other than their past-life memories, with nearly three quarters of those showing just a slight amount. If the past-life memories are examples of psychic abilities, those abilities are for the most part oddly limited to the memories and perspective of one specific deceased individual.

A FIRE ON C STREET, PART II

I sent the above write-up to Kathleen to check for any errors in my telling. She wrote back that Nicole, now seven, picked up the printout of the story and began reading out loud. When she read "A Fire on C Street," she yelled, "Yeah, that's how it was spelled!" She made little comments as the family read it but none that seemed heartfelt until they came to the mention of Virginia City, Nevada. Nicole grabbed the paper and said, "Let me see that. Where did you say that was?" Kathleen answered

Nevada. Nicole repeated "Nevada" and then started yelling, "Nevada, that's it! That's it! It's Nevada! We have to go to Nevada!" Kathleen tried to put her off, but Nicole persisted, saying, "Mom, that's it, that's it!"

I was surprised by Nicole's reaction, because she wasn't really talking about C Street anymore. Given her positive response to Nevada, I suggested we go to Virginia City to check it out. It would be expensive, with four of us flying there, but a generous donation we had received a few months before meant we had the funds to undertake the trip.

Kathleen responded hesitantly but said that if it might be beneficial to Nicole to go at some point, she would welcome the opportunity. I told her that if we were going to go, we should do so before Nicole got any older since the memories in these children usually fade. We also discussed the potential effects of a trip on Nicole, both positive and negative. When the family talked about it, both Kathleen and Lynn were unsure, but Nicole was emphatic about going. She told Kathleen, "Mom, what are you guys afraid of? What do you think might happen?" Kathleen told her she was afraid that C Street wouldn't be as she remembered it. Nicole said she understood that was possible but kept repeating that she needed to go.

And so we went to Virginia City. We were corresponding over the summer, and though it made sense to go before Nicole started back to school, August is not necessarily the most pleasant time to visit Nevada. The trip did not result in any definitive discoveries but did have some interesting parts.

I met Nicole and her mothers at the Reno airport. Our flights were supposed to arrive at the same time. As my connecting flight was rolling down the runway, however, an alarm went off in the cockpit because of a mechanical problem. After a long delay to determine if the issue could be resolved, the airline eventually found another plane for us, and we finally flew to Reno. This made me hours late to meet Nicole and her parents, who were stuck at the airport waiting for me. Nicole and Kathleen put the time to good use by taking a long nap, and they were all understanding about the delay.

I hadn't seen Nicole for four years, since she was three years old, and yet she seemed to remember me. After a brief initial period of shyness, she was very friendly and outgoing. We got the rental car and then took quite a winding road to Virginia City. As we rode on the asphalt surface, Nicole at one point said, "They didn't have these black roads when I lived here before." Because of the flight delay, it was near the end of the day by the time we got to Virginia City, and since we had the whole next day to explore, we just had dinner and called it a day. The inn where we stayed was made up of three different buildings, at least one of which was built before the fire in 1875, but Nicole showed no particular reaction to it.

The next morning, it was time to explore. We had explained to Nicole that we were trying to determine if Virginia City was the place she remembered, but that since the fire was a long time ago, things would look different now than they did back then. Virginia City had been a boomtown in the late 1800s because of mining. It began with mining for gold. After workers complained of all the blue mud that would stick to their shovels, some of which was used to pave streets, someone figured out that the blue was due to silver. Silver mining then became a huge operation there. Those days are long gone now, and the city has a population of under a thousand people. It's still a tourist attraction, though, and some people remember it as the town the Cartwrights frequented on the *Bonanza* television show.

It turns out that C Street is the center of activity in Virginia City and always has been. We learned that there were some small houses and some boarding houses there before the fire, but it was also the major commercial street. We started at the visitor center, which was located on C Street. Nicole had talked a lot about a church that was near her house. There was the Presbyterian church on C Street that had been the one church in town left undamaged by the fire. It was a few blocks from the visitor center, so we walked down to it. I saw no way to disguise what we were doing, so I simply asked Nicole if this was the church she remembered. She said it was not; the church she remembered was more pointed at the top. Being right in front of the church, the top of it was hard to see from her vantage point. We walked across the street so we could see it better. It had a small steeple at the top, and from the new angle Nicole said, not very convincingly, that it might be the one she remembered.

Nicole had also said the church was on a corner, which this one was not. I soon noticed another church that was just off of C Street. It was a large, more ornate Catholic church that had a sizable steeple. As we approached it on a town tour, Nicole said, "They did a good job of repairing it. It looks almost like it did before." After the tour, we walked back to the church. Nicole had told her parents that her father got married in a church that took up a whole block. This church was indeed that large. She had described her father in a black suit, dancing at a wedding, and her parents had the sense she was talking about the wedding when he married her stepmother.

We went inside the church and its impressive sanctuary. We learned that the wooden interior had been destroyed in the fire but that the exterior walls were the original ones from

1868. Nicole had mentioned a church near her home a number of times. She had said it was on a corner and that it hadn't burned down in the fire. It wasn't clear if those descriptions were of the same church where her father was married, but this church could fit all the details. Nicole didn't show any obvious reaction to it. Inside, I asked her if this was the one she remembered, but she didn't respond. Throughout the visit, in fact, she was reluctant to discuss any memories, particularly with her parents.

We went to a museum to learn more about the town's history. We found out that when the mines were being created, special wood frames were designed for the tunnel interiors to keep them from collapsing. This led to a tremendous need for timber, but there were no forests right by Virginia City. As a result, lumber mills were built where the forests were, and the lumber was transported from the mills to the mines. Water pathways or flume were constructed on which the wood could be floated to the city. The longest flume was nearly twenty-five miles in length, and by 1879, there were eighty miles of flume in the Sierra. That year, more than thirty-three million feet of lumber were transported by flume. At the museum, we saw pictures of a lumber mill and a large flume. Nicole's talk about her father floating trees in water thus fit for Virginia City, much more than it would for most places. It was an odd detail, but one appropriate for that area.

Another detail that fit for Virginia City involved horses. Nicole had talked about horses that would walk through town and into her yard. She said that boys would chase them and try to jump on them to ride them. That sounded like nonsense to Kathleen and she dismissed it. We learned in Virginia City that wild horses had been in the area for a long time and are there to this day. In fact, we saw one walking through town.

One detail Nicole had given that I had largely dismissed was a name she pronounced O'Manny. That sounded made up to me, but Nicole said that a friend who lived next to her had that name. Kathleen discovered online that the Irish surname O'Mahony is pronounced O'Manny. (I also learned later that a reality television personality had the name Ommanney, as did Admiral Erasmus Ommanney in the British Royal Navy.) There was a large Irish population in Virginia City, which also fit with a comment Nicole had made when she was younger. She said her sister had taught her how to put on makeup and had also taught her how to hooley dance. Kathleen didn't know what a hooley dance was (and neither did I), but *hooley* is an Irish word that the *OED* defines as "a noisy party." Another source describes it as an evening of traditional music and dance.

Kathleen and I decided to check out the Irish cemetery for any O'Mahonys. I initially suggested taking Nicole to the cemeteries to see if any names were familiar to her. She wanted no part of that, and once Kathleen and I visited the Irish one, I was glad Nicole wasn't with us. In the ninety-five-degree Nevada heat, we had a long walk past various cemeteries just to get to the Irish section. Once there, we discovered a sprawling collection of graves on uneven ground, some that were hard to get to and some that appeared completely untended. We did not see any O'Mahonys, and after a long, hot search, we were both happy to make it back to the car more or less intact.

Throughout the trip, Nicole was an engaging, happy seven-year-old. She didn't appear to have any emotional reactions to the sights we saw, though admittedly many things looked different that they did over a hundred years ago. We did not find definite evidence that Virginia City was the place of her memories. It was consistent with her statements in a fairly striking way at times, but I couldn't be one hundred percent sure it was the right place. Nicole had no such doubts. Her one show of emotion came at the end of the trip. Kathleen related to me that as the family's plane was lifting off from the Reno airport, Nicole suddenly burst into tears. She said, "I don't want to leave here. This was more than just a trip." Kathleen asked if she really thought Virginia City was her home before, and Nicole responded, "No, I *know* it was."

Though none of the cases in this chapter conclude with an identification of the previous person, they are good examples of this phenomenon. It is not just some strange thing that happens in faraway places—these cases have occurred in typical American families, most of whom say they had no belief in past lives before the children started reporting their memories. And these are just the tip of the iceberg, as we've heard from scores of other families reporting similar events. Families may not tell many people about them, but they are happening nonetheless.

When I was in private practice, I once treated a boy for attention-deficit/hyperactivity disorder. I later learned that his family had previously contacted Ian because the boy was talking about a past life. They hadn't told me, his treating psychiatrist, about it, so I'm sure they kept it from a lot of people. The parents in some cases haven't even told the child's grandparents about the statements because in our culture, they can sound pretty weird. So even if you never hear about it, your neighbors or co-workers or distant family members may have a child who talks about a past life. That doesn't mean the child has given details that can be traced to one deceased individual. But after hearing story after story after story, I've become convinced that we should take such reports seriously.

Chapter 8

MIND OVER MATTER

After studying the cases I have and reviewing the notes of Ian's investigations, I have concluded that some young children do appear to possess memories and emotions that come from a deceased individual. How does a reasonable person make sense of this? Something extraordinary seems to be going on, but how can an idea like past lives mesh with the world of science and all that we have learned through the scientific method?

The answer lies in being aware that science involves more than just scientific materialism, the concept that the world consists entirely of physical matter. On the basis of materialism, most mainstream scientists would dismiss the cases out of hand because they say that no part of us can continue after our bodies die. As I've learned more about scientific knowledge as it exists today, however, I have discovered that the picture is actually much more complex.

Findings in physics over the last hundred years—particularly in quantum physics or quantum mechanics, the study of the universe's smallest particles—have shown that the physical universe is much more complicated than it appears. They strengthen my view that there is a consciousness that exists separate from the material world. I now believe that the physical grows out of the mental, meaning that the physical world is created out of something you can think of as Mind or consciousness or the spiritual. Our cases, and the possibility of children remembering past lives, then fit in nicely with a new understanding of existence.

Materialism—the belief that physical matter is all there is—has become practically synonymous with modern science, and it is unquestioned by many, though certainly not all, scientists. It relegates religion to antiquated folk belief and consciousness to purely a product of a physical brain. Any consideration of the nonphysical is akin to a belief in fairies or leprechauns.

Modern science was not always so certain of materialism. Isaac Newton, one of its founders, wrote numerous religious tracts. Alfred Russel Wallace, the co-discoverer of the theory of natural selection with Charles Darwin, was impressed by séances he attended and publicly advocated spiritualism. Many other scientists open to religious or spiritual ideas could be mentioned as well. The point is that the worldview currently presented by mainstream science that the physical universe is all there is conflicts with views that many esteemed scientists have held.

Such views continue to be held quietly by a minority of scientists today. A recent study found that a quarter of scientists from top research universities regarded themselves as spiritual, which many viewed as separate from religious. Even twenty percent of the atheist scientists considered themselves "spiritual atheists." Many of the scientists in various fields who are religious tend to keep their faith—or in some cases, their other anomalous beliefs—separate from their scientific outlooks, and private as well. There are exceptions. Francis

S. Collins, the geneticist who served as director of the Human Genome Project and is currently the director of the National Institutes of Health, wrote a book entitled *The Language of God: A Scientist Presents Evidence for Belief*, pushing for harmony between science and religious faith. Brian Josephson, a Nobel laureate physicist, created a controversy when his contribution to a booklet accompanying a set of stamps that commemorated the one hundredth anniversary of the Nobel Prizes included a statement about developments that "may lead to an explanation of processes still not understood within conventional science, such as telepathy."

What most mainstream scientists seem unaware of, or at most only vaguely aware of, is that the most fundamental findings of physics have now disproven materialism. Valuing a special place for consciousness or spirituality can be incorporated into an overall understanding that includes the insights gained through science. Work in quantum mechanics has undermined many of the basics of what we thought we knew.

When the findings of Newton and others in classical physics explained so many of the world's happenings so well, it was logical to conclude that they were all that was needed to understand everything in the world, from the smallest particle to the largest galaxy. Then came relativity and, with perhaps even more paradigm-shattering effect, quantum mechanics. As Henry Stapp, a physicist at the Lawrence Berkeley National Laboratory, has said, "We have known for almost a century that this theoretical creation of the human mind called 'classical physics' is a fiction of our imagination." Classical physics is a close approximation of reality, in most cases one of such remarkable accuracy that it is sufficient for all practical purposes. But while classical physics works most of the time, the inferences that we draw from it may not be correct. And in fact you will see that one of these—materialism—has now been shown to be wrong.

The universe gives the appearance that it sprang into existence approximately 13.8 billion years ago. According to the Big Bang theory, all matter and energy present in the universe today began then as a single point. They expanded with the Big Bang to create the still expanding universe of today. After 300,000 years or so, hydrogen and helium molecules began to form. Another 300,000 years later, clumps of matter formed and began coalescing into galaxies. Our sun was formed around 4.5 billion years ago, and the planets followed after that.

By appearances, eukaryotic cell organisms developed one and a half to two billion years ago, followed by multicellular life. More complex organisms developed, leading eventually to the variety of plants and animals present today. Humans were the accidental result of natural selection. As their brains evolved, their frontal lobes grew and produced the experience of consciousness. As conscious observers, humans were eventually able to examine the world and learn how it came into existence.

I now believe this story is seriously incomplete. Consciousness is not merely an incidental byproduct of evolution. The logical conclusion from various findings in physics is that consciousness actually creates the universe. And its creative process continues to occur in every instant. As Max Planck, a founder of quantum theory, said, "I regard consciousness as fundamental. I regard matter as derivative from consciousness. We cannot get behind consciousness."

Work in quantum mechanics has revealed what is known as the measurement problem. This unassuming name describes a challenge that shakes our understanding of the world to its core. Quantum theory says that particles on the small quantum scale exist less as solid objects and more as probability waves. Only when an object is measured, it seems, does its probability wave collapse to produce one outcome.

Being aware of the critical role that measurement—or more to the point, observation—plays can lead to new understandings about the true nature of the world, ones that are both more wondrous and more accurate than the previous mechanistic view of the universe. To get to those, I need to take a detour into the world of physics, which I now believe provides crucial insights about the spiritual realm and the ultimate nature of reality. Despite any rough terrain along the way, you'll see that the destination is worth the trip.

TURNING THE PROBABLE INTO THE ACTUAL

There is a frequently cited work in physics called the double-slit experiment, which I touched on briefly in my first book. In the experiment, you have a light source, along with a photographic plate that records the light that's emitted. Between them, you place a screen that blocks the light. If you cut a slit in the screen for the light to pass through, then a fuzzy image is created on the photographic plate that corresponds to the location of the slit.

What happens if you cut a second slit in the screen? You might think you would get two fuzzy images, matching the two slits, but you don't. Instead, the light appears to pass through the slits as waves, producing an interference pattern on the photographic plate, of alternating light and dark bands. An analogy would be the waves you get if you throw two large objects into a lake. Where waves from the objects collide, you get a large peak in the water, whereas two troughs combine to produce a deeper depression, and a wave from one and a trough from the other cancel each other out. It's not water waves in the double-slit experiment, but light waves seem to come out of the slits and interfere with each other, producing this pattern of light and dark bands.

Light sometimes acts as if it's made up of particles called photons, and other times it acts like waves. But here's the thing about the double-slit experiment: when you turn down the light source so low that the light goes through the screen one photon at a time, guess what happens? Somehow, you still get the interference pattern. As Paul Dirac said, "Each photon then interferes only with itself." It's as if each photon hasn't made up its mind which slit to choose and goes through both of them simultaneously.

In case you think these results are simply due to the strangeness of light, its particle-wave duality, you should know that the double-slit experiment has now been done with electrons as well. In fact, similar experiments have been done with neutrons, atoms, and even larger molecules. Not just light but actual matter also acts like waves, seeming to go in two places at once and interfering with itself.

The famed physicist Richard Feynman said the double-slit experiment was "impossible, *absolutely* impossible, to explain in any classical way" and it "has in it the heart of quantum mechanics." I hope I've conveyed just how strange the results are. Particles act like waves, being in two places at once. But waves of what, exactly? It now appears that matter should be thought of as waves of probability.

Most of us learned in science class that atoms, the building blocks of the universe, consist of electrons circling a nucleus like small billiard balls. Quantum physicists tell us instead that electrons are better seen as smears of probability, with their locations being potentials rather than definite places. As strange as it may seem, it is only when an electron is measured that its location goes from a smear to a specific spot.

In the double-slit experiment, there is one thing that can force the photons to make up their minds and go through one slit or the other. If you set up sensors to observe them as they travel, each photon is seen going through just one of the slits. The interference pattern on the photographic plate disappears, and you get two fuzzy images corresponding to the two slits instead. The observation leads to one path, one definite outcome, rather than the two potential outcomes that existed before.

Similarly, take a small particle that can travel down one of two paths, with a fifty-fifty chance of going down each one. According to quantum theory, until someone looks to see which path it goes down, with a measuring device for instance, all that can be said about the particle is that it has the two probabilities. Common sense says it goes down a path but we just don't know which one until someone checks. Common sense, however, can be misleading at the quantum level. Until the particle is observed, it does not actually go down either path. It simply exists as a fifty-fifty probability wave for going down each one.

To say that light and matter only exist as probability waves until they are observed raises the question of what existence in such a state would mean. As Werner Heisenberg, one of the founders of quantum physics, noted, "The atoms or the elementary particles themselves are not as real [as any phenomena in daily life]; they form a world of potentialities or possibilities rather than one of things or facts." With a measurement, one outcome snaps into place. "The transition from the 'possible' to the 'actual' takes place during the act of observation," to quote Heisenberg again. The measurement somehow causes one of the two possibilities—or in other situations one of many possibilities—to become the reality that is seen. Measuring something thus creates a reality that did not exist before.

The findings from the double-slit experiment are an example of superposition, the idea of a particle being in multiple states simultaneously. This concept applies not only to the location of particles but to other attributes as well, such as velocity and spin. In all of these, multiple possibilities exist. Heisenberg called the potential outcomes *potentia*, and all the potentia add up to produce a probability wave. A photon may go through one slit or the other, and both possibilities coexist as superpositions of possibility. When a photon, or an electron, is detected, the probability wave reduces down to the one outcome that is observed. It is only with measurement that the various possibilities are collapsed down to one actuality, and physicists refer to this as the collapse of the wave function.

A MEASUREMENT OR AN OBSERVATION?

When a measurement produces an outcome, is it the change in the measuring device that collapses the wave function, or does it collapse when the scientist observes the result? One person who considered this question was John von Neumann, a brilliant mathematician who wrote a book called *Mathematische Grundlagen der Quantenmechanik* (*Mathematical Foundations of Quantum Mechanics*). It provided, as its title said, rigorous mathematical foundations for the theories of the quantum physicists. Physicist Nick Herbert calls it the "quantum bible" and says that like many sacred texts, it is revered by many but read by few (the latter perhaps because it is filled with an astounding number of mathematical equations).

In the book, von Neumann discusses how the world must

be divided into two parts, the observed system and the observer. He shows that where we consider the cut between the two can be in various places. The measuring instrument can be considered part of the observed system or part of the observer; the mathematical result is the same. In fact, the changes in the retina of the observer as he looks at the measuring instrument can be considered part of the observed system. Even the chemical changes of his brain cells can be considered part of the observed system, until all that counts as the observer is "his abstract 'ego.'" The one essential part of the observer—in the critical interaction of observed system and observer that produces events in the world—is the observer's abstract ego, or "the intellectual inner life of the individual." No result in a measurement actually occurs until, as Herbert summarizes, a physical signal in the brain becomes an experience in the human mind.

Another guide to this question came from physicist Mauritius Renninger. He produced a thought experiment that involves finding a negative result. For an example that's simpler than Renninger's original, imagine that you do an experiment in which a photon can take one of two paths, and a measuring device can be set up on one of the paths to determine if the photon goes down it. The device failing to detect it on that path would mean that the photon must have taken the other one. As Renninger and others examined this situation, they found that observing the absence of a photon on the first path collapses the wave function just as much as observing the presence of it would. Since nothing is actually measured and only an absence is observed, this indicates that the observation—not the measurement itself—is the critical process in wave function collapse. As Johns Hopkins physicist Richard Conn Henry wrote in the journal *Nature*, "The wave function is collapsed simply by your human mind seeing nothing." This led him to conclude, "The Universe is entirely mental."

Experimental evidence along these lines has come from the world of parapsychology. Researchers have used devices called random number generators or random event generators that produce output in a completely random pattern. For example, a device might put out a series of light flashes, either green ones or red ones. There would be a fifty percent chance each time of the flash being either red or green. In studies, people then try to use their minds to change the output in one direction or the other so that more red flashes or more green flashes are produced than you would expect by chance. A considerable amount of data using random event generators has indicated that willful conscious effort can indeed cause a slight but significant deviation in the output of the devices so that it's no longer random.

A researcher named Helmut Schmidt, who was a physicist as well as a parapsychologist, took the work a step further to see if conscious effort could produce nonrandom results *even if the effort occurred after the events had already been recorded.* He got positive results in the five studies he did, with odds against chance of 8,000 to 1. He recorded random events such as the red and green light flashes, and the series of flashes was then stored on a floppy disk. Days or months later, the sequence was shown on a computer while a test subject tried to mentally cause one of the colors to flash more. As long as no one inspected the recordings beforehand, the mental efforts of the test subjects could cause the results to be nonrandom, with more of one color appearing than would be expected by chance. The test subjects' success means that the collapse of the wave function did not occur when the flashes of light were initially measured by the recording device; it only happened when the recordings were later observed. French physicist Olivier Costa de Beauregard wrote that the experiments "may herald a scientific revolution akin to the Rotating Earth one."

Thus, Renninger-type experiments show that observation can collapse the wave function even when nothing physical is actually measured. Schmidt's research demonstrated that interaction with a recording device fails to collapse the wave function; the collapse only occurs when the result is later observed. Von Neumann was therefore right that a change in a measuring device is not the critical factor. It is the awareness by the observer that appears to complete the process and produce a single reality out of the various possibilities.

It also seems that it's not the observing per se that produces a result, it is the knowing produced by the observing that does. By seeing that a particle doesn't go down one path, an observer in the Renninger-type experiments can deduce that it must have gone down the other one. Since no other result is possible, the observer "knows" which path the particle took, thereby collapsing the wave function and producing the result. It is not the act of measuring that produces a result, it is the act of knowing—the interaction of the world with von Neumann's "intellectual interlife of the individual."

THE LARGER WORLD

If you're telling yourself that all this weirdness is just limited to the tiny quantum world, then you're mistaken. You're in good company, to be sure, as physicists for a long time thought that while quantum mechanics ruled the microworld, classical physics controlled the larger one. They assumed there was some kind of border between the two. But not anymore. Few physicists would still give classical physics equal billing with quantum mechanics. Classical physics is a useful approximation, but the world is ultimately quantum at all levels.

Physicist Brian Greene has written that quantum mechanics "shows that the universe is founded on principles that, from the standpoint of our day-to-day experiences, are bizarre." These principles must extend beyond the microscopic quantum world since quantum events can have macroscopic consequences, as large objects can be dependent on the quantum behaviors of their atomic parts.

This effect of the quantum on the larger world is colorfully exemplified by Schrödinger's famous cat. Intending to show the absurdity of quantum theory's dependence on measurement, Erwin Schrödinger suggested a thought experiment in which a cat is put in a chamber with a vial of poison, a hammer, and a small amount of a radioactive substance. A device is set up so that the decay of a single radioactive atom will cause the hammer to fall, breaking the vial, releasing the poison, and killing the cat. There is so little of the radioactive substance that over an hour, there is only a fifty percent chance that an atom disintegrates and sets off the device.

If the contraption is left alone for an hour, the atom is in a superposition of both having decayed and having not decayed as long as it remains unobserved. This would mean that the cat is also in a superposition of being simultaneously both dead and alive—not the kind of result you want your theory to produce. One might conclude from this that quantum mechanics fails when systems get large enough or complex enough. Experimental findings now show, however, that superposition can indeed occur with macroscopic objects. A paper in the journal *Nature* in the year 2000 showed that an instrument called a superconducting quantum interference device (or SQUID) could be put in a superposition of two states simultaneously: one with current flowing clockwise and the other with current flowing counterclockwise. This led to commentaries with titles like "Schrödinger's SQUID," "Schrödinger's cat is now fat," and "New life for Schrödinger's cat." Work has advanced to the point that physicists at University of California, Santa Barbara, achieved superposition in an object that's even visible to the naked eye. After *Nature* published their study, the journal *Science* named it the Breakthrough of the Year for 2010.

Quantum effects can be present in the larger world, even if they are hard to see. As physicist Anton Zeilinger has said, "A transition from quantum to classical as you go from micro- to macroscopic . . . is not going to happen in my expectation. It's just a question of the skill of the experimenter and how much money [there is] to perform the experiment." Numerous experiments, from Zeilinger and others, have now demonstrated quantum effects in increasingly larger objects, and it appears clear that there is no definite border between the two worlds. The world at the quantum level and the larger one at the classical level are not two separate systems. Even though it's usually not apparent, the larger grows out of the quantum with all its strange patterns.

OBSERVING THE PAST

The quantum world not only can affect the larger one, it can even affect the past. Observation in particular is necessary to determine the past. Recall the double-slit experiment, in which light particles travel through two slits at once unless observation forces them to go through one or the other. John Wheeler, a notable figure in physics who among numerous other accomplishments gave black holes their name, imagined a thought experiment in which the double-slit experiment is done with a twist. You have the sensors set up to observe the photons going through the slits as before, but you also have a barrier that blocks the sensors from "seeing" the photons and the slits. If you leave the barrier up, the photons seem to go through both slits simultaneously and produce an interference wave pattern. If you lower the barrier, the sensors measure the photons, which then go through one slit or the other as discreet particles.

Wheeler suggested that you could wait and lower the barrier just after the photons went through the slits. The sensors would observe the particles as they continued to travel, producing definite paths coming from one slit or the other. In this way, the decision of whether to lower the barrier would determine if the photons were acting like waves or particles when they passed through the slits—even though that decision wouldn't be made until after they did. Thus, the decision would determine what kind of path the photons had taken as they went through the slits *in the past*.

This kind of delayed-choice experiment has now been carried out experimentally by several groups. They confirm that the later choice determines the earlier behavior of the photons.

Wheeler wasn't content to stop there. He advanced his line of reasoning to near mind-boggling proportions when he proposed a similar thought experiment on a galactic scale. Imagine a distant quasar that is emitting light. Between it and Earth would be two large galaxies, whose gravity could bend the light as it headed toward Earth. In this huge version of the double-slit experiment, the quasar would be the light source, and the galaxies would substitute for the slits. Astronomers on Earth could point telescopes at the galaxies to observe light photons as they were deflected by the galaxies. Or, they could set up mirrors in such a way that photons deflected by the two galaxies would not be observed but would instead hit a piece of film, producing the alternating light and dark bands produced by waves, even if the quasar was so far away that light from it would hit the film one photon at a time. The alternating interference bands would mean that the photons had seemingly traveled through both galaxies simultaneously, even though they would be light-years apart.

More amazing still is that since this would just be a really large version of the double-slit experiment, it would be the astronomers' actions that determined the kind of path the photons took. The astronomers would force each photon to go through one galaxy or the other if they observed it with a telescope as it did so, or the photons would act like waves, going through both galaxies simultaneously and producing the alternating bands on the film. Since the quasar would be so far from Earth, however, the photons would have begun their travels billions of years before.

Observers on Earth could thus determine the kind of path that a photon started *billions of years before*. They could do this, not because they reach billions of years into the past, but because the probability wave function for that path, even the part of it in the long ago past, does not collapse until an observation is made. The wave function, consisting of all the possible paths the photons could have taken, continues to exist even for billions of years, until an observation finally collapses it and produces one outcome. Another way of saying this is that the histories of the photons aren't determined until they are known by observers.

BECOMING ENTANGLED

Another example of the interplay between knowledge and time is the concept of entanglement, a problem that has puzzled physicists for nearly eighty years. Albert Einstein was unhappy with quantum theory in 1935. It held that attributes of particles were just potentials until one outcome was observed. Einstein felt this must be wrong, that the attributes existed before they were observed, they were just hidden. He published a paper with two young colleagues, Boris Podolsky and Nathan Rosen, based on discussions they had about a thought experiment, with Podolsky writing the manuscript. Einstein was subsequently unhappy with the particulars of the paper itself, and it's not clear he even read the final draft before Podolsky submitted it.

Even so, this little paper—not quite four pages long, without references, and with its famous author dissatisfied—has had a profound impact on the course of physics, being cited in physics journals far more than any other paper Einstein ever wrote. It is known simply as EPR, the initials of its authors. The setup of the EPR thought experiment usually cited today is an alternative proposed by David Bohm, since Podolsky's original fairly obscured its central point. In the Bohm version, two particles interact in a way that causes them to have opposite results for a given attribute; for instance, if one particle is "spin-up" the other is "spin-down." After that interaction, the particles go in different directions. When someone later measures the spin of one of the particles, the spin of the other one is automatically known since the two spins are opposites.

Einstein thought EPR proved that quantum theory was an incomplete description of reality. It said that the spin of the particles only becomes definite when a measurement is made. Further, the theory said that no matter how far apart the particles go, measuring the spin of the first one would cause the spin of the second to suddenly snap into existence, even though the two particles would be completely separated by a great distance.

The EPR authors pointed out that the experiment would make the reality of the second particle "depend upon the process of measurement carried out on the first [particle], which does not disturb the second [particle] in any way." They then stated, "No reasonable definition of reality could be expected to permit this."

Perhaps that means that reality is not reasonable, because as subsequent events have demonstrated, that turns out to be the way the world is. John Bell published a discussion of EPR in 1964 that led to this realization. Bell's theorem takes two assumptions. One is that objects have separability: in Bohm's EPR example, the assumption is that measuring the spin orientation of one particle doesn't affect the orientation of the second particle in a remote location. The other assumption is that objects are real: the second particle had a predetermined orientation before the first particle was measured. Bell showed mathematically that any theory that exactly reproduced the predictions of quantum mechanics would violate one of the two assumptions. Thus, any interpretation based on realism would have to be "grossly non-local."

Following Bell's paper, experiments using entangled pairs of particles were carried out, most notably by Alain Aspect and colleagues, but by others as well. The setups for the actual lab experiments were different than the Bohm EPR example, but the principles were the same. The results were consistent with quantum mechanics and not with local reality, demonstrating that EPR does not show that quantum theory is incomplete. Instead, EPR led the way to the discovery that the idea of a local reality is incorrect.

Bell wrote that requiring locality—requiring that measuring one particle wouldn't affect the distant second particle—was the essential problem. But that was only one assumption in his theorem. The other one—requiring a physical reality to exist before any observation—could instead be faulty. Though such a possibility appears more consistent with the rest of quantum theory, it seems so illogical that many physicists have tended to avoid addressing it. Bruce Rosenblum and Fred Kuttner are two physicists who, despite being open to considering consciousness alongside quantum physics, recently wrote about Bell's theorem, "Our world therefore does *not* have both reality and separability. (And we immediately admit to having little understanding of what the world being unreal might mean.)" Even so, the nonlocality explanation has recently been falling out of favor.

In 2007, a group of physicists in Vienna published a study in *Nature*. They conducted a Bell-type experiment, except in this case, it relied only on realism and not so much on locality. They found that just assuming realism—that there is an objective reality separate from observation—would still produce results that differed from quantum mechanical predictions and from those that occurred during the experiment. The study thus refuted realism, leading the *Physics World* Web site to produce a headline proclaiming, "Quantum physics says goodbye to reality." The researchers couldn't exclude all classes of nonlocal theories but felt their results indicated that any nonlocal extension of quantum theory would have to be "highly counterintuitive." And if you don't accept a nonlocal explanation, you're left with the denial of objective reality.

This leads to a way to understand entanglement that was first proposed by Costa de Beauregard back in 1953. In EPR, an interaction produces opposite spins in two particles. Whether the spin of each of them is up or down isn't known until one of them is measured in the future. More important, not only are the spins not known, they aren't even real until one of the particles is measured. Likewise, the original interaction that produced the opposite spins isn't real either; it remains a collection of ghostly potentia until the results of it are known.

When the spin of one of the particles is eventually observed, it becomes definite. This causes its previous interaction with the second particle, when it acquired its spin direction, to become definite, too, because the interaction had to go in a particular way to produce that outcome. With the original interaction being definite, the spin of the second particle becomes definite as well, since it was also established in that interaction. The observation thus produces not only the present of the particles (their spins), but their past as well. Making the past definite, by looking at the spin of one of the particles, creates the illusion that measuring one particle suddenly affects the other one a great distance away. It does in a way, but only because it affects the particle's past. Entanglement occurs because the initial interaction between the two particles that created their opposite spin directions doesn't become actualized—the wave function doesn't collapse—until an observer later measures the spin of one of them.

A MATTER OF TIME

Entanglement makes clear that until their outcomes are known, *events in the past haven't happened yet*. With his theory of special relativity, Einstein showed that time is not the constant it seems to be. Two clocks moving through space at different speeds will tick at different rates, meaning that time as we think of it can move at different rates. The findings of quantum physics lead to a conclusion that time is even stranger than that. In essence, until the results of an event are known, it hasn't really happened yet, even though it may occur on a date we think of as being in the past.

Events do occur in a timeline but not necessarily in order. I can draw a timeline with four events on it labeled A through D:

My common sense tells me that Event A happens first, then Event B, then Event C, and then Event D. Quantum physics tells a different story. It says that Event A doesn't occur until its outcome is known, so Event B could actually happen—it could become definite when its wave function collapses—before Event A does. If I place myself at the end of the timeline and say that I'm at the present, Event A from what seems like the distant past may not have even happened yet. It may still only be a number of potential outcomes.

If the terms weren't so ingrained in our minds, it might be more accurate to think that events whose outcomes have been observed (or are at least known) are in the past, events being observed now are the present, and events that have not yet been observed are still in the future. Those "future events" could be anywhere along a timeline, from the year 2525 to the year 1776 to the time when photons from a distant quasar began their paths toward Earth. Some people talk about backward causation or retrocausality, of reaching back in time to change a previous event. But observing previous events doesn't change the past—because the unobserved past hasn't happened yet.

There is a well-known paradox about time travel, that if such a thing were possible, a time traveler could go back and kill his grandfather before he had fathered children, thus preventing the time traveler from existing in the first place. (But since he then wouldn't have existed to go back, his grandfather would still be alive, and on and on. Stephen King dispensed with the paradox in his recent time-travel novel *11/22/63* when one character is talking about going back in time and another one asks what would happen if you went back and killed your grandfather. The first character stares at him baffled and asks, "Why the [heck] would you do that?" and the conversation moves on.) With the model I'm describing, the existence of the time traveler means his grandfather definitely lived to have children, so that part of his life couldn't be undone (its wave function has already collapsed). I'm not talking about going back into a past that's happened; I'm saying that events that we think of as occurring in the past don't actually happen until observation creates a particular outcome. As Wheeler wrote, "It is wrong to think of [the] past as 'already existing' in all detail. The 'past' is theory. The past has no existence except as it is recorded in the present."

There is no limit to how far in the past events can be and still be undetermined. Remember that Wheeler pointed out that how astronomers choose to make measurements on Earth can affect the path a photon takes to get here—even the path it took billions of years before the astronomers were around to make their measurements. He wrote that since equipment operating in the present plays a part in bringing about things that appear to have already happened, the idea that the world exists "out there" independent of us can no longer be upheld. He wrote that "in some strange sense this is a 'participatory universe'" and that "there is a sense in which what the observer will do in the future defines what happens in the past— even a past so remote that life did not then exist." He added that quantum physics shows that "'observership' is a pre-requisite for any useful version of 'reality,'" saying this leads one "to explore the working hypothesis that 'observership is the mechanism of genesis.'" Observership is the mechanism of genesis: that's quite an idea, that the observer is the creator. Wheeler suggested that "acts of observer-participancy" could give "tangible 'reality'" to even the beginnings of the universe.

Despite appearances, the universe was not created in one fell swoop in the Big Bang. Instead, it continues to be created, one observation at a time. Events in the distant past such as the paths of photons billions of years ago—even events all the way back to the Big Bang—remain in suspended animation until they are observed, at which point one particular outcome occurs. Stanford physicist Andrei Linde has said, "You may ask whether the universe really existed before you start looking at it. . . . And my answer would be that the universe *looks* as if it existed before I started looking at it. . . . When we look at the universe, the best we can say is that it looks as if it were there 10 billion years ago."

This does not mean that we human observers had to come into existence. Different life forms might have evolved here or in other places in the universe. Observers had to develop somewhere, however, in order for the world to exist. This idea explains how the universe appears so finely tuned to support life. If some of the physical constants or initial conditions of the universe had been different, not only would life have been impossible, planets couldn't even have formed. Some have argued that the odds of a low-entropy universe with formed matter, not to mention intelligent life, are so infinitesimally small as to be almost zero. Since such a universe does in fact exist, some people say it is evidence for the existence of God. There are two responses against this. The first is that any universe we could be in would obviously have to be able to support life. The second is a concept called the multiverse, the idea that there could be an infinite number of universes that bubble into existence, so many that very rarely one would occur that could support life. Thus, there is nothing miraculous about our universe being the way it is.

With Wheeler's genesis through observership comes a different view, which is known as the strong anthropic principle. A universe that supports the development of observers is the only kind that ever *could* come into existence. The universe, our universe, was only in a state of countless potentia until observation caused a past to snap into existence, and that past clearly had to be one that would eventually produce observers. As Wheeler said, "Unless the blind dice of mutation and natural selection lead to life and consciousness and observership at some point down the road, the universe could not have come into being in the first place, according to the views under exploration here." There might have been nothing rather than something perhaps, but since "something" has to be observed before it can exist, a universe has to have observers. There are no lifeless, empty universes, because such a universe could never be observed into existence.

It might seem that humans on this little planet, or observers anywhere in any galaxy, are far too small and unimportant to have any significant function in the universe, much less bring it into existence. Observation, however, couldn't create a smaller universe, not because of size per se but because of the time required to produce life. An observed universe would have to be old enough for there to be elements other than hydrogen, since as Dicke said, "It is well known that carbon is required to make physicists." This is not entirely humorous, since the measurements by physicists to determine the age of the universe help determine that age. As Wheeler pointed out, to produce heavy elements like carbon out of hydrogen, thermonuclear combustion is required, and it needs several billion years to cook inside a star. And for the universe to provide several billion years of time, general relativity says it must extend in space several billion light-years. Any observed universe would have to be as big as ours is, in order to have observers. Though our tiny size in relation to the enormity of universe may make living things appear insignificant, tiny living things can't produce a universe that's any smaller. And the universe can't exist without tiny living things to observe it.

THE WORLD OF CONSCIOUSNESS

Wheeler resisted the seemingly obvious connection between observation and *conscious* observation. He was quick to say that " 'consciousness' has nothing whatsoever to do with the quantum process," which involves only an event making itself known by being registered or recorded in some way. He did add that if that record then enters into someone's consciousness and is the first step in giving the measurement meaning, then that part of the story is important, but is not a "quantum phenomenon."

Others have not been so reluctant to consider consciousness in the quantum process. The issue started with von Neumann's mathematical work I described earlier. Though he only hinted at a consciousness-created reality, others have been more straightforward about it. Eugene Wigner, a Nobel laureate, proposed a thought experiment that came to be known as Wigner's friend. In it, a light may or may not flash at a given time. Wigner sets up a device in which, for example, an atom is excited if the light flashes. If he is out of the room, the wave function for the event does not collapse until Wigner comes back and checks the device. If instead of the device, Wigner's friend is in the room seeing if there is a flash, the wave function must collapse before he tells Wigner whether he saw one. It collapses when the friend observes the flash; otherwise, he would be in suspended animation until he gave Wigner the result. Because of this difference, Wigner wrote that "the being with a consciousness must have a different role in quantum mechanics than the inanimate measuring device." He said "it is the entering of an impression into our consciousness which alters the wave function" and that "it is at this point that the consciousness enters the theory unavoidably and unalterably."

The ideas of von Neumann and Wigner led to the Consciousness Causes Collapse (of the wave function) school of thought. One person identified with it more recently is Berkeley physicist Henry Stapp. He has written books with titles such as *Mindful Universe* and *Mind, Matter and Quantum Mechanics*. Stanford physicist Andrei Linde has also said, "I do not know any sense in which I could claim that the universe is here in the absence of observers. We are together, the universe and us. . . . I cannot imagine a consistent theory of everything that ignores consciousness."

Back in the 1930s, Sir James Jeans, a well-known British physicist and astronomer, made the oft-quoted statement, "The universe begins to look more like a great thought than like a great machine." He added, "Mind no longer appears as an accidental intruder into the realm of matter; we are beginning to suspect that we ought rather to hail it as the creator and governor of the realm of matter." French physicist Bernard d'Espagnat has written, "The doctrine that the world is made up of objects whose existence is independent of human consciousness turns out to be in conflict with quantum mechanics and with facts established by experiment."

I quote the various scientists to show that these ideas are part of mainstream physics. Since it has been said that there are as many interpretations of quantum theory as there are quantum physicists, I don't mean to say that this is the consensus view, or even the majority opinion. At the same time, these ideas are not merely New Age woo-woo physics. When a giant such as von Neumann points in a particular direction, it warrants serious consideration.

I hope I've shown that these ideas are a natural conclusion of the findings in quantum physics. If you think they are wild, you should hear some of the alternatives. One of the leading explanations proposed for the measurement problem is Everett's many-worlds interpretation. It says that when a measurement is made, the wave function doesn't collapse and produce one result. Instead, all possible results occur, each in its own parallel universe as the world branches into different versions of itself. The observer only sees one result, but other versions of the observer see the other possible results. The branches have no effect on each other, so no observer is ever aware that the split occurred.

Since every measurement creates separate universes in this hypothesis, the "many" in many-worlds quickly becomes a gross understatement. "An infinite number raised to an infinite power" might be more accurate. Yet this idea is taken seriously by a lot of physicists as a way to keep the observer out of quantum theory.

Wheeler's stated reason for denying the importance of consciousness, and I suspect the reason for many physicists, is that he saw it as one more physical process. He believed that "brain function"—the mind—"will someday be explained entirely in

terms of physical chemistry and electrochemical potentials."
This materialist worldview meant that Wheeler could see the
importance of the observer—he had astounding insights about
how observation could even create the distant past—but he was
unable to accept that the consciousness of that observer was
critical.

There is a paradox here to be sure. As Wheeler said, quantum mechanics leads us to consider the idea that "the observer
is as essential to the creation of the universe as the universe is
to the creation of the observer." Conscious observers eventually
evolved in the universe . . . and then created that very same
universe. How does that make sense? One answer is that individual observers are the result of evolution, it's true, but that
doesn't mean that consciousness itself is. For people like me
who are open to the possibility that consciousness is more
than just the result of physical chemistry and electrochemical
potentials—that there might be more to existence than just the
physical universe—the way out of the paradox is for consciousness to be primary. The physical world grows out of it. The findings of quantum physics have challenged the worldview of
materialism from the outset; at the very least, they have unde-
niably shown that the world does not function at the smallest
level in a way that common sense suggests it does. The findings
point, not just for me but for a number of physicists as well, to
the fundamental importance of consciousness. Something has
to be outside the quantum system to register it, to observe it.
My answer is that consciousness is outside the quantum system, interacting with the physical universe but also existing beyond it, as it registers and creates that universe. Consciousness
does not exist because the physical world does; the physical
world exists because consciousness does. As Max Planck said,
we cannot get behind consciousness.

A SHARED DREAM

The picture that emerges from quantum physics is a world in which events do not occur until conscious beings observe them. One way to comprehend this is to realize that it is quite similar to another world we know very well—the world of our dreams. When we are dreaming, people only come into existence there when we interact with them. They snap into existence the instant we observe them. Otherwise, the various people from our waking lives exist only as possibilities in the backs of our minds, figures who could exist in our dream world but so far remain mere potentials. Even though we are not aware of the similarity as we experience our lives, quantum physics has shown that the physical world works in the same way.

There are differences, to be sure. All sorts of nonsensical things happen in the dream world. We can suddenly fly in some dreams, but we are unlikely to do so in the physical world. It is undeniable that the possibilities are more limited in the physical world. Events that begin through observation become fixed, unable to be altered by other observations. The overall process, however, is very similar. Possibilities exist, and one of them becomes a fact when it is observed.

The analogy to dreams is so apt that the world can be thought of, not as the giant clockworks of Isaac Newton's mechanistic universe, but as a dream that all its observers share. Its pieces only come into existence when one of its dreamers experiences them. When something is not being observed, it may as well not exist.

Becoming aware that the universe at its most basic level depends on consciousness in order to exist requires us to alter our understandings of the world. The findings in quantum mechanics are so startling and, frankly, so hard to comprehend, that many scientists in other areas have not yet incorporated them into their fields. Biologists, for example, still tend to think of consciousness as being simply a byproduct of the brain as it evolved to help organisms survive in the natural world—an epiphenomenon, as it is called.

This view needs to change. A more accurate understanding is more optimistic: the universe is not a purposeless place that we came to exist in by random accident. Consciousness is the primary force of existence, and the physical universe is secondary to it. It exists because we exist, a product of our group imagination. We think of our minds existing in this world, but it's actually the world that exists in our minds.

We are the physical beings living in a physical world that mainstream science tells us we are. But we also have consciousness that is more than just a product of our brains. Though we have physical bodies with limited life spans, we also have a conscious piece that is part of something bigger. Consciousness is independent of the physical world and even the creator of the physical world. And a portion of it is in each of us.

Seeing that the world is like a shared dream can help us understand more about the interaction between mind and matter in our lives. In my dreams, I can't control what happens or what other people are doing. But some people do develop more control over their dreams. They have what are known as lucid dreams, in which they become aware they are dreaming. They then have more ability to shape what happens.

Perhaps we can develop more control over the physical world in the same way. Gertrude Schmeidler was an experimental psychologist working at Harvard in 1942 when she found repeatedly that people who rejected any possibility of psychic abilities did worse on ESP tests than people who were at least open to the idea. This finding has since been confirmed by numerous other researchers and has been termed the sheep-goat effect (with nonbelievers being the goats). What people believe is possible helps determine what is indeed possible for them, and being aware of the mental foundation of the world may open us up to new possibilities.

One possibility that I hope you are now open to is the prospect of life after death that our cases of past-life memories suggest. Each of the children seems to have a consciousness that existed before in another person. Though this may seem ludicrous from a materialist standpoint, the situation gets much more interesting when we take the findings from quantum physicists into account. If the physical universe grows out of consciousness, there is no reason to think that a person's individual consciousness ends when the physical brain dies. It may continue after death and return in a future life.

Chapter 9

WORKING ON A DREAM

Being open to the possibility of life after death naturally makes me curious about what it might involve. With the idea that the world exists as a shared dream, my thinking about it has changed. I no longer imagine that we go to another place when we die. Instead, we have another dream. The idea of some entity—a soul or a consciousness—moving from one world to another places too much emphasis on the physical worlds. Instead, the new experiences continue to be creations of the mind. If the shared dream model is correct, there need not be just one afterlife. Each individual starts another dream at the point of death, and the nature of the dream can vary from person to person.

EXPERIENCES NEAR DEATH

The immediate dream often seems to be a transition dream, involving an awareness of dying and moving on to another kind of existence. Near-death experiences (or NDEs) are, as the name suggests, the events that people report having when they come very close to death before being revived. I mentioned earlier the details they report, of floating above their bodies, going through a tunnel to another place, and often having a life review, seeing deceased relatives, and encountering a being of light.

The specifics of these experiences can vary. Just as people's nighttime dreams are affected by their previous experiences, I would expect afterlife events to be affected by experiences in life, and this seems to be the case. In particular, though there are common features of NDEs across cultures, there are also cultural differences.

Allan Kellehear reviewed reports of NDEs that had been published from a number of countries. Looking at the parts of NDEs that are common in the Western cases, he found that the major features seen across cultures were going to other worlds and encountering other beings. The tunnel experience was not reported in any of the non-Western NDEs, though times in darkness were often described. An out-of-body experience was present in the NDEs of most cultures, and the life review was present in several.

Satwant Pasricha likewise found both similarities and differences between accounts of NDEs in India and ones in the U.S. Both Indian and American subjects reported meeting dead relatives and acquaintances, seeing religious figures or beings of light, being revived through the thoughts of loved living persons, being sent back from the other realm by a loved one, and seeing their own physical body while seemingly dead.

She also reported features of Indian NDEs that were not seen in American ones, as the Indian subjects often told a different narrative from the typical American experience. Many of the Indian subjects described being taken to another realm by messengers, who then passed the subjects on to Yama, the god of death. When Yama's book containing a list of deeds and misdeeds was opened, it was discovered that the messengers had brought the wrong person. Someone else was due to die, not the subject, who then came back to this world and lived.

Todd Murphy collected ten NDE cases from Thai popular literature. The imagery people reported seemed to be culturally influenced, though Murphy argued that it should actually be considered a reflection of the individuals' expectations of what death would be like rather than their culture per se. The themes he reported were Yamatoots (the messengers Pasricha described in the Indian cases), the importance of merit accumulated during life, and, as in the Indian cases, the presence of cases of mistaken identity. The universal features pointed out by Kellehear and Pasricha were also present in the Thai NDEs. For example, dead friends and relatives were seen in four of Murphy's ten cases.

The overall message from these reports is that people from many parts of the world who come close to death describe having experiences as their bodies are in the process of dying. Such experiences seem to occur everywhere, but the ones people have are certainly not identical. Some people take the differences to mean that NDEs are not real events and that they do not provide evidence that consciousness can exist independently of the brain. Author Sam Harris recently made this argument regarding an NDE that Eben Alexander, a neurosurgeon for many years at Harvard Medical School, experienced and then wrote about in his book, *Proof of Heaven*. Harris noted that Alexander's account differed from another recent one, that of a four-year-old boy described in the book *Heaven Is for Real*, commenting that Alexander doesn't mention that Jesus rides a rainbow-colored horse or that souls of dead children must still do homework in heaven.

The fallacy of Harris's argument is that it's based on the premise that, as he says, "if a nonphysical domain were truly being explored, some universal characteristics would stand out." As I've just described, some universal characteristics do stand out, but beyond that, the bigger issue is that there is not just a single place where people go after they die. With the model I'm presenting, differences would be expected when people experience their next consciousness-created reality, their next dream. Just as an American Christian is unlikely to dream at night about Yama, the god of death, and an Indian Hindu is unlikely to dream about Jesus, a four-year-old's next consciousness-created reality may have little in common with that of a neurosurgeon.

The differences in the reports do argue against there being one afterlife place where everyone goes, as Harris says. But I would argue against that, too. The reports of NDEs from different people and different places show the variations I would expect to see. It appears that expectations and experiences play a role in the next reality that a person encounters (or helps create), just as our experiences and thoughts prior to going to sleep can shape our nighttime dreams.

The distinct differences among the experiences of various individuals also argue against the idea that NDEs are merely the result of the firings of dying brains, which might be expected to produce more uniform images. Arguing against this as well are the reports that many of the past-life children make about events between lives. About twenty percent of the children say they remember either observing earthly events such as the previous person's funeral, going to another realm, or having experiences related to conception or gestation to begin their current life.

Poonam Sharma, a medical student who worked with us one summer before heading to great things in internal medicine, compared published NDE reports to the children's descriptions in our cases of the time between lives, looking particularly at the Burmese cases she was coding for us to include in our database. She found significant overlap. For the Western NDEs, this was especially true for the transcendental aspects. For NDE reports from other parts of the world, the universal features of NDEs were seen in the children's intermission descriptions. The Burmese intermission reports were similar, though not identical, to the NDE reports from neighboring India and Thailand. These similarities indicated that the intermission memories need to be considered part of the same overall phenomenon—reports of the afterlife—that includes NDEs.

American children also describe memories of the time between lives that sound very much like NDEs. Patrick, the little boy in Chapter 1, reported encountering a relative in heaven—"Billy the Pirate," who was upset that no one talked about him after his death—in the same way many NDE patients describe seeing deceased relatives. Likewise, just as NDE patients report going to another realm, Lee, the boy who seemed to remember Sidney Coe Howard's life, described being in a castle up in the clouds somewhere. He said the castle didn't have lights or a potty, but it did have windows. When his mother asked how he went from a castle up in the sky to being Lee, he said he climbed down a ladder to become Lee. Though a castle in the sky may seem rather fantastic, it could have been part of the dream world Lee experienced before reentering this dream world, what we think of as reality.

The idea that NDEs are merely the product of the final firings of dying brains, which some people offer as a way to explain them, can't possibly work for these similar reports from healthy, young children. The intermission reports also weaken the argument that people who have NDEs create fantasies of an afterlife as a defense to avoid confronting the end of their existence. Our cases involve young children who have not been close to death and in fact usually aren't old enough to fully comprehend the concept of death, yet their reports can be quite similar to NDE reports—thus posing a problem for psychological explanations offered for NDEs. Both phenomena—near-death experiences and intermission reports from young children—may in fact be glimpses of the afterlife, and they are both consistent with the model of consciousness-created reality.

THE DREAM CONTINUES

With the past-life memories they report, the children in our cases seem to be returning to the world in which they lived a previous life. A better way of describing this is to say that regardless of whether the children have an intermission experience, they fall back into the same dream they were in before—meaning this world. They have to be a new character as they continue, since the previous person has died in the dream at that point. Imagine that you are sleeping at night; you are awakened in the middle of a dream—perhaps you are startled awake by something traumatic that happens in it—but then you fall back asleep quickly and continue on in the same dream. This is completely analogous to what happens in our cases.

First, the new life usually starts very soon after the last one ended. The median interval—meaning half the cases have a shorter interval and half have a longer one—between the death of the previous person and the birth of the child is only sixteen months. Though most of the cases in this book are exceptions, the interval is typically very short. Thus, these cases are like waking up from a dream and then falling back asleep quickly and continuing in the same dream.

The endings of the past lives tend to be like dreams that end prematurely. In seventy percent of our cases, the previous person died by unnatural means, either by murder, suicide, or accident. James Huston's death in the Pacific and Sidney Coe Howard's fatal tractor accident are typical examples. The previous individuals also tend to die quite young, with the median age at death being only twenty-eight years old. Even when the previous people died from natural causes, their median age was only thirty-five, with a quarter of those deaths occurring when the person was fifteen or less. Thus, the death of Patrick's half brother at age two is unusual in the general population, but not so in our cases.

If you look at a graph of the number of deaths in the general population by the age when people die, what you see is a curve that gradually slopes up as more and more die with each older age group. In our cases, even when you look just at ones in which the previous person died naturally, what you see is the reverse, with the curve sloping down:

AGE OF PREVIOUS PERSON AT DEATH BY NATURAL MEANS

Dying young increases the likelihood that a child will later report memories of your life. With the model I'm proposing, this makes sense. Individuals whose dreams end prematurely—by being brief or through an abrupt ending—are more likely to return quickly to the same dream. Meaning, people who die young or by unnatural means are more likely to return to our mind-created world to start another life.

This idea of returning to the same dream also explains another pattern. The previous person was from the same country as the child in over ninety percent of our cases, often having lived fairly close by. Even when the child talks about a deceased individual from a different country, there is usually a connection with the child's country, such as Burmese children who have talked about being Japanese soldiers who were killed in Burma during World War II. If an individual resumes the same dream with a new life, it seems logical that the circumstances would be fairly similar to the original ones. He or she can't return as the same person since the previous individual died in this dream, but usually comes back in the same general area.

Emotional connections or unresolved emotional issues may affect where the individual comes back in the dream. If you compare cases in which the previous person was a deceased member of the child's family with ones in which the families were complete strangers, you find that there are some statistically significant differences regarding how the previous person died. Cases involving ordinary deaths are more likely to be same-family cases. The families are more likely to be strangers when more exceptional deaths were involved, meaning when the previous person died an unnatural death, died younger, or died unexpectedly even when the death was from natural causes.

My interpretation of this is that individuals with strong or unresolved emotional connections to their families—such as Patrick's half brother with his mother Lisa—come back to the same dream to continue the story with them. In situations without those emotional issues, these other factors—the unnatural or early or unexpected deaths—cause the individual to quickly fall back into the same dream as before, but not necessarily into the same family.

OTHER WORLDS

With our nighttime dreams, it's unusual of course to return to the same dream. I wonder if that's the case with our lives as well. Past-life memories, as far as anyone can tell, are not common. Only one systematic survey has been done looking at their frequency. It involved people in one section of India, and the researchers found that one case occurred for every 450 inhabitants, though they acknowledged they may have missed some cases. It's at least conceivable that many more children come into the world with past-life memories but that they either lose the memories before they are verbal enough to convey them or that their attempts to convey them are ignored or rebuffed strongly enough by their parents to quash them.

Nonetheless, there is no evidence that most children have such memories and thus no evidence, even if you accept our cases, that everyone is reborn back into this world. I see no reason to think that other mind-created worlds, other shared dreams, wouldn't exist in addition to the world we know here. Just as we don't usually return to the same dream when we sleep at night, the same pattern may well be true for our lives. Though individuals occasionally return to this shared dream, it might be more common to begin participating in a different shared dream after we die.

What might these other consciousness-created worlds be like? I suspect that depends on the experiences we've had in this life. Our nighttime dreams are certainly affected by our experiences during the day. The themes of your day may repeat themselves in your dreams at night. If you watch a horror movie, you may regret doing so later when you have bad dreams. Your experiences matter; they affect the dreams that follow.

Likewise, your life experiences could affect the mind-created worlds that follow after you die. Many Christians say your actions or beliefs determine whether you go to Heaven or Hell. But if I am right about existence being like a shared dream, then there might not be just one Heaven or just one Hell. There might be an infinite number of shared dreams, some heavenly, some hellish, and some like this world—heavenly at times, hellish at times, and most of the time somewhere in between. I do find it notable, however, that in this model I'm suggesting, the religions are right that the decisions and actions you make in this life help determine the kind of existence you have next. Though this would not involve a Judgment Day of any kind, you could experience a "good" afterlife or a "bad" one based on your life now, in what would be a purely naturalistic process.

This process also seems similar to karma, the Eastern concept that your actions determine your future circumstances. I don't mean karmic retribution or any sort of orchestrated punishments or rewards, but there could be consequences that would flow naturally from your prior experiences. Tibetan Buddhists feel that in addition to how you live your life, the state of mind you are in at the moment of death—your last thoughts and emotions—are critical in determining the existence you have next. This would be consistent with this model in which what your mind creates next is affected by the thoughts that lead up to each moment.

The afterlife environment might be surprisingly similar to this one. Though we don't typically return to the same dream at night, our dreams usually involve a fairly similar setting. There could be differences, to be sure, perhaps as many as the mind can imagine, and the physics might be distinctly different in one world compared to another. But at the very least, I think there would still be a space-time kind of experience and not purely thought or spirit. For there to be a sequence of events—for things to happen—there has to be, it seems to me, some kind of space-time world.

An illustration of this comes from the mediumship literature. Mediumship, the idea that certain individuals can communicate with the deceased, is a topic for another book, or really a library full of books. Suffice it to say that a number of renowned scientists such as William James and a couple of Nobel Prize winners tested mediums a century ago and concluded that some of them had access to information through some extraordinary ability of the mind, material that appeared to come from the deceased. (The researchers also found that many other mediums had no talent at all.)

Numerous descriptions of the afterlife were given by mediums, but the example I want to share comes from Reverend C. Drayton Thomas, or more precisely from his deceased wife. Reverend Thomas wrote books about mediumship in the 1920s and '30s. Our office has a photocopy of a rough-draft manuscript he wrote at some point. It includes various corrections, some handwritten. I don't know that it was ever published, but at the end is a three-page description that really struck me. Entitled "An account of her passing given by my wife through the mediumship of Mrs. Osborne Leonard," it purports to be a description by Thomas's wife of events in the afterlife. It concludes with "What I am so astonished about is the reality and substance of things here. . . . In the garden I . . . tried feeling the trees, and found that their bark felt just as solid as the trees in our garden at home. I even tried to shake the trees but could not; they were large trees and felt firm to my hand. When I touch other people their hands, too, feel firm. There is nothing vague or vapoury about us."

I don't think there is our world and then the real spiritual world. Our world is as real as it gets. It is created by Mind, but that is also true for all other worlds. Existence grows out of consciousness. I don't think, for example, that reality is like the movie *The Matrix*, where human beings interact in a computer simulation of the world, completely unaware that in actuality they are in constant sleep in pods while machines use their bodies as energy sources. The world is indeed like a mind-simulated virtual reality, in a way, but it's as real as reality gets.

Who is with us in the shared dreams of the afterlife? When I dream at night, people who are meaningful to me tend to pop up repeatedly. Characters in my dreams include people who are around me a lot—my wife, of course, as well as friends or co-workers—along with people I happened to run into during the preceding day or even just had occasion to think about that day. But then there are also those I haven't seen or thought about for some time but with whom I still feel an emotional connection. This is particularly true for people I've known, or even pets I've had, who are deceased, some of whom I've dreamed about periodically for years after their deaths. I may dream about them even more than I did when they were alive, because their absence leaves an emotional tie that can no longer be fulfilled.

Our consciousness-created worlds may be populated in a similar way. Certainly the initial ones are, as people who have near-death experiences often report seeing deceased relatives on the other side. (Some even report seeing deceased relatives they hadn't known were dead before they had their NDEs, producing some very impressive cases.) I would hate to think of getting to the afterlife and not being able to see my loved ones again, and I think those connections would cause them to be with me again in the next world. Eventually the emotional ties may be resolved so those individuals would no longer be present, but my emotional need initially would keep them with me, causing them to appear in my next shared dream.

It's unclear how time would work across mind-created worlds. It's easiest to conceptualize lifetimes as being sequential—first I have one life, then another, then another—but I don't know if that makes complete sense when the lives involve different dream worlds. The different worlds or different dreams—while being space-time worlds—would themselves transcend space-time. While I think any world where things happen has to involve space and time, I'm not sure they would have to follow each other sequentially. They certainly appear to in some instances, such as when people report encountering other realms in NDEs. But I suspect the process is complex. For example, perhaps individuals can be characters in more than one dream. Perhaps you will see your deceased grandmother after you die one day, while "at the same time" she has also been reborn into another life here. Things may not be linear in a way we can easily understand.

Other examples of when one dream seems to follow another occur when children say they watched events in their parents' lives from heaven, such as James Leininger recalling his parents' trip to Hawaii or Ryan describing his mother's reaction when her ultrasound revealed she was having a little boy. These are a bit more challenging to explain with the dream model. They suggest individuals may occasionally be able to see across dreams or worlds, to view one dream while experiencing another one. This would be similar to reports in mediumship, where individuals in the afterlife—in a different dream—appear able to communicate with individuals in this world. At times, some people seem able to cross boundaries of consciousness. I make no claim to fully understand how they do it, but this ability may illustrate that consciousness and consciousness-created realities are more fluid and interconnected than we might think.

THE DREAMER

If we can move from one dream to another when we die, then some part of us would transcend the worlds we experience. We would have a larger self existing across our lives. To go back to the dream model, I exist as a character in my nighttime dreams, usually my daytime self but occasionally someone else. Along with my character in the short-lived dream, I as a dreamer also have my real self that exists apart from the dream. Like-wise, I think we each have a larger part of us that transcends the individual dream—the individual lifetime—and continues to take part in creating other dreams, other lifetimes or worlds.

I suspect our roles in life are much like an actor's roles in movies. As we go from one life to another, or more accurately have one dream and then another, our characteristics in each life may vary quite a bit. We have different traits in each life, affected in this world by our genetic makeup and our upbring-ing. But a larger aspect of each of us would also carry over from one life to the next. Jimmy Stewart played many charac-ters during his long acting career—most of them nice, some not so nice, some simple, some complex—but regardless of the character, it was always unmistakably Jimmy Stewart who was playing the role. There was this entity, this actor, who existed in each of his characters but also existed outside of them. The same might be true for us across lives. There would be a larger entity than just the person—or going back to the second chapter, the snake—we were in our previous life.

Jimmy Stewart brought something that informed and shaped each character he played. A character played by Jimmy Stewart turned out differently than one played by Cary Grant. I suspect the same holds true for any multiple lives we lead, that our consciousness brings something unique to each life. We start a life with a tendency for certain traits or patterns.

We have some evidence in our past-life cases that supports this. Among the variables we code for each case in our database, we include six personality or behavioral items for both the child and the previous person. (They were established a long time ago and may sound a bit archaic.) They are: Is/Was the person attached to wealth? Does the subject show a tendency toward criminality, and was the previous person a criminal? Is/Was the person philanthropic or generous? Is/Was the person active in religious observances? Does/Did the person meditate? Is/was the person saintly?

We don't have this information for most of our cases, so only a small number are included in the analysis for each item. Even so, there is a statistically significant correlation between the amount of every feature in the previous person and the amount in the child, meaning the more the previous person showed a feature, the more likely the child is to show it as well. This correlation is strong enough for each of the features so that the odds of it occurring by chance are no more than one in a hundred. The personalities of the two people are not identical by any means—we know genetics and environment have a large impact on personality development—but there does seem to be an effect. Certain tendencies have carried over.

I also suspect that not only does the individual bring something to each life but that each life also informs the individual, just as our experiences shape our development in this life. This larger self is not static but can change or grow. In this way, each individual does make progress (or at times may fall back) in what can be called spiritual development. My view is that this occurs in a natural way, not through some orchestrated effort. I don't believe that between lives, individuals meet with guides or some sort of council to learn what issues they will work on in their upcoming lives (as some hypnotic regression proponents suggest). Some individuals may have dreams like that before beginning this dream, but I doubt the true process is so literal. Rather, our next lives, whether in this world or another, will involve previously unresolved issues, just as our nighttime dreams are attempts by our minds to process unresolved emotional material.

To speculate about an example, a person who focuses on hoarding his wealth in one lifetime may have a "nightmare" in his next life in which he is poor. Over the course of several lifetimes, he may come to see that wealth is not critical to having a satisfying life, so it will fade as an issue for him. As we make progress through some of our patterns, those will fall away, and we will move on to work on others. Progress is thus made as the content of each "dream" evolves. This seems similar to how species on Earth make progress when they evolve through natural selection. Just as the accidental changes in species ultimately lead to ever more successful adaptations to the environment, there may be side steps or steps in the wrong direction, but with the dream content changing as issues are resolved, spiritual progress is ultimately made in a naturalistic way.

Working through issues may involve difficult experiences, and certainly some people endure terrible pain and suffering in this life. On a smaller scale, we experience difficult events in nightmares as our minds attempt to process various emotions in our unconscious. Likewise, I hope that the traumas people suffer in life are part of a working-through process that across lifetimes may ultimately lead to resolution and progress.

MIND AND LIFE

One big difference between our nighttime dreams and our life experiences is that in our dreams, the other characters don't have an internal existence. They only exist because we observe them. In life, every conscious being presumably has an internal existence (unless you want to fall into solipsism and decide you're the only one who really exists). We are all co-creators of this shared dream, not our characters or personalities, but the conscious part of us that transcends the particular dream, the particular lifetime.

How might the larger part of each of us—the Dreamer—be connected to the other dreamers? In looking at the way our world works so seamlessly—once I observe the outcome of an event, the result is set for any future observers—I think the unique consciousness in each of us must be part of a larger whole. Each of us is contributing to a tapestry of existence rather than creating our own individual work.

The I in my nighttime dreams, my character in the dreams, is part of a bigger I, my larger mind out of which my dream world arises. All the people in the dream are arising from the same consciousness, in the case of my nighttime dreams, from mine. In the same way, all the individuals in the physical world may also arise from the same consciousness, from some larger conscious force.

Work that may be relevant to this came from Carl Jung. He explored the connection between the mental and the physical with his concept of synchronicity or meaningful coincidences, which involves correspondences between mental images and objective situations. He included three types of synchronistic events. The first is the one people usually focus on. In it, the mental state of an observer corresponds with a simultaneous external event in a meaningful way. He shares an example from his psychotherapy work with a woman who was too rational and intellectual to fully engage in therapy. As she was telling him one day about a dream in which she was given a golden scarab, an expensive piece of jewelry, Jung heard a tapping on the window behind him. He opened it and grabbed the insect that flew in. It was a scarabaeid beetle, whose gold-green color made it as close to a golden scarab as anything in that part of the world. He handed it to the patient and said, "Here is your scarab." The incident helped them push through her defenses and led to more productive psychotherapy.

Bernard Beitman, a friend and colleague of mine, has recently been studying synchronicities and coincidences. He points out that Jung was an active agent in this story. Not only did he get up and take the beetle to the patient, but Bernie feels Jung's emotions were important in producing the events, that his frustration with the patient's intellectualizing somehow helped cause that beetle to appear.

Jung's second type of synchronicity was a coincidence between a mental state and a corresponding physical event taking place away from the observer. An example he gave was when Emanuel Swedenborg had a vision of a great fire that was burning at the time in Stockholm, 250 miles away. The third type was a coincidence between a mental state and an event in the future that can only be verified later. With this, he discussed J. B. Rhine's ESP studies in which subjects guessed a series of cards that were not laid out until minutes or even weeks after the subjects made their picks. The results of the experiments showed odds that the subjects' correct answers occurred by chance were only one in 400,000.

With all of these, Jung argued that there was no physical cause that could have conceivably produced them, that they were "acausal." He said that, along with the connection between cause and effect, synchronicity was another factor in nature that the arrangement of certain events demonstrated. He noted that it could be dependent on the affective state—the mood—of the observer, that a positive state of faith and optimism led, in the ESP tests for example, to better results.

Bernie also related a story from another writer on coincidences, Roderick Main, about a man who was intensely studying the Biblical Book of Zechariah, in which Zechariah has a vision of four horsemen whose horses are red, black, white, and dappled. The man took a break, walked out onto the balcony of his hotel room, and saw four horses below: a red one, a black one, a white one, and a dappled one. He was stunned.

When Bernie told the story, I suggested the explanation for it involved affecting the collapse of a wave function, that the man's focus on the imagery of four horses of different colors had increased the likelihood that four horses of different color might separate themselves from other horses grazing nearby and end up by his hotel balcony. This would be producing one outcome from a fairly random group of possibilities, and the repeated imagery of the horses would be analogous to focusing on a particular scene one day and then dreaming about it that night.

Bernie's reaction to my suggestion, as I recall, was to laugh. And he is certainly right that this would not be a simple case of collapsing the wave function like observing an electron to see which slit it goes through. But I do think some similar interaction between inward consciousness and outward physical events could be involved.

An example in my own life points out that this idea of a connection may be applied more broadly to other events, but also that the connection is complex. When I was fervently trying to get my first book published, I sent query letters out to numerous literary agents, including one to Patricia van der Leun. What I didn't know at the time—what I couldn't have known at the time—was that Patricia had just had a conversation with one of her authors, B. Alan Wallace, a scholar of Tibetan Buddhism and president of the Santa Barbara Institute for Consciousness Studies. Alan, whom I only met later, told Patricia about Ian Stevenson's work here at the University of Virginia. She was therefore intrigued when she received my letter soon thereafter. She asked me to send a book proposal, which she then took with her to a lunch she had planned with an editor at St. Martin's Press, Diane Reverand. Diane liked the proposal, so before I knew anything about it, I was close to having a publisher. In fact, we got an offer from St. Martin's before Patricia and I had even signed our agent/author agreement. And so the book was on its way.

You can decide I was simply lucky. But if you consider that consciousness may be involved in apparent luck, these events demonstrate what a complex process it can be. My wish to find a publisher didn't make Alan Wallace devote many years of his life to the study of Buddhism or hire Patricia as his agent. It didn't cause Patricia and Diane Reverand to be friends or create Diane's interest in such topics, as she had served as editor for a number of books on near-death experiences. The pieces nonetheless all fit together to create an outcome that was quite meaningful to me. Jung would not have counted this as a synchronicity, because the series of events was not so unlikely that they couldn't have occurred by chance. But I am struck by the possibility that the connection between the goal in my mind and a series of events that occurred largely out of my control involved something more than chance. This would not necessarily mean that my wish produced the outcome exactly, but consciousness may have been involved—in some complex way—in creating the physical reality that resulted. If so, this suggests that our thoughts—the images in our minds, our wishes and goals—are linked to each other's and to outcomes in the physical world. These thoughts and the subsequent realities may not only be linked but may emanate from the same source. In that way, the various pieces from my series of events in finding a publisher—or from the golden scarab story or the four horse story—fit together because they are all coming ultimately from one Mind.

This doesn't necessarily mean that everything that happens is planned or intended by this Mind. I don't control or plan the events in my nighttime dreams, and I know my mind creates those. The physical world may work the same way. This consciousness-created reality may include painful or negative events that happen randomly without any conscious intent or control. Even so, we may be able to reduce them by appealing to the benign aspect of this larger Mind.

If I accidentally touch a hot object, I am not burning my

hand to make it stronger; the event was just incidental. My immediate reaction is to move my hand away. The nerves from my fingers instantly send pain impulses to my central nervous system, which reacts quickly to send nerve impulses back to my arm telling it to move my hand. Each of us may be like a single nerve cell in one large nervous system, so every thought made with intention such as a wish or prayer may be like a pain sensation reaching the brain. Though the brain and the larger organism may or may not respond to the pain signal, there would be a natural tendency to remove the negative sensation, just as we do with our own bodies. At times, however, people override uncomfortable sensations—of pain as they are working out, or cold as they are traveling outside in the wintertime, for example—for their larger overall goals. So it might be with existence, that what looks from our individual, close-up perspectives like negative sensation we wish we could avoid—such as pain or disappointment—might help us make progress in the long run, just as an aching muscle during a workout becomes bigger and stronger over time.

I have no idea why my wish to get a publisher might have effected that outcome when similar goals in other circumstances do not. The world doesn't seem to function as Rhonda Byrne's book *The Secret* describes, with its idea that positive thoughts work as powerful magnets to attract positive outcomes like good health and great wealth. If only life were that simple. I do think that our hopes and wishes can affect outcomes, that we may be able to produce change by applying conscious intention to the world's happenings—it's just not as easy or straightforward as *The Secret* makes it out to be. I think exploring how to increase this effect—through prayer, meditation, insight, or as Jung's writings on synchronicity suggest, a state of faith and optimism—could be useful if the goal is to have more control over the events in this consciousness-created existence. We can try to improve the dream and make this a better world. At the same time, our hopes and wishes may be able to do only so much to override the creation—or perhaps the plan—of the Ultimate Source of both consciousness and the physical world. Religious people sometimes pray, "Thy will be done," which is a way to appeal to the benign aspect of this larger Mind, along with a recognition that there may be much that we do not understand.

THE BIG PICTURE

Since part of us seems able to transcend the various dream worlds as we move from one to another in different lifetimes, there must also be existence outside of these worlds and out-side of space-time—an existence of pure Mind. Each of us may be like a single train of thought in one large Mind. We seem to be like a chain of islands as William James suggested, sepa-rate when seen above the water but connected at the ocean floor. More than just connected, islands turn out to be projec-tions that are so many small parts of a single larger object, the planet. Likewise, each of our minds may turn out to be small streams of consciousness that are all part of a larger Mind, a "cosmic consciousness" as James said. This is not to deny our individualism; each island in the sea is an individual thing. But it is also part of something bigger.

In the same way, we may exist as individuals on the sur-face, while being part of something much bigger. Bigger than we can conceive, since we are not considering one sea but rather all thought. Imagine every train of thought you have had in your life multiplied by the billions of people who have lived on this one planet in this one galaxy multiplied by thoughts from countless other dream worlds, and suddenly the cosmic consciousness seems far bigger than even the physical cosmos.

Beneath the waterline of our individual existences, we may be part of this endless consciousness, something I am tempted to call the Mind of God. This is a far, far cry from my Southern Baptist roots, and yet this infinite realm of thought from which all worlds, all emotions, all events from the coalescence of a new planet to the fading glow of a dying star, from the first breath of a newborn baby to the final sigh of a long life well-lived flow, this Ultimate Source of all existence must be the thing that our feeble minds can only comprehend in some shrunken, anthropomorphized, clouded facsimile we call God. We think we can make out the vague outline, but the enormity of the thing makes it so much greater than we can imagine.

I know this is a long way from children's past-life memories. But as each step has followed the other, this is where the journey has led. A little boy who repeatedly relives the exact details of the terrible death of a young World War II pilot challenges the mainstream understanding that consciousness is always created by—and confined to—a physical brain. Exploring quantum physics then produces a way to understand such events because it leads to a rational conclusion that the physical world grows out of consciousness, meaning that consciousness must not be limited by the physical. A child in Louisiana remembering events from the life of a pilot from Pennsylvania offers a glimpse that consciousness survives across lifetimes and that experiences separated by great distances and many years can nonetheless be connected and intertwined.

This connection, along with the seamless way in which observations from countless observers create our holistic world, indicates that a single individual consciousness is only a tiny piece in the act of creation, that all the pieces work in concert as part of a bigger whole, and just as our physical world grows out of consciousness, so the entirety of existence grows out of this bigger whole, this Ultimate Source. As mere streams of thoughts from one large Mind, we are not separate; we are all in this together. And just as our experiences in life can enrich our individual minds, if this awareness that we are all part of the Ultimate helps us be a little more patient, a little more accepting, a little more loving, if it helps us to focus more on our shared experiences and less on our differences, then perhaps in some small way, we will be better able to enrich the Ultimate and, with it, all of existence.

Acknowledgments

I am very grateful to the families described in this book, for sharing both their stories and their time with me. Needless to say, *Return to Life* would not have been possible without them. I have changed most of their names, but fortunately, they know who they are.

The trips to Asia I discuss in Chapter 2 would clearly have been fruitless without the able help of translators, Sutdya Vajrabhaya and Wichian Sittiprapaporn in Thailand and U Myint Aung in Myanmar.

I also want to thank Greyson and Ariana Williams. Their generous donation enabled me to dedicate more of my time to completing the book. It also funded the research trip described in Chapter 7.

Patricia van der Leun, my literary agent, and Daniela Rapp, my editor at St. Martin's, helped make this a much better book than it would have been otherwise. Copy editor Eric Meyer added numerous improvements. Suggestions from Lori Derr and David Sauvage were also quite helpful.

Finally, I want to thank the love of my life, my wife,

Chris. She has again served as my unofficial editor. More important, being with her continues to energize my exploration of life and my appreciation of what it has to offer each and every day.

Notes

CHAPTER 1

p. 10: Ian had previously determined: Stevenson, 1993.

p. 10: *Reincarnation and Biology*: Stevenson, 1997.

p. 11: a man who vividly recalled: Moody, 1946.

p. 12: Carol Bowman: Bowman, 1997 and 2001.

p. 13: "If the vapid writings": Stevenson, 1978, p. 323.

p. 13: In a review of one of his books: King, 1975.

p. 14: We eventually included: Pasricha, et al., 2005.

p. 15: it published a letter: Stevenson, 1999.

p. 15: One was from Tom Shroder: Shroder, 2008.

p. 15: wrote a book about them: Shroder, 1999.

p. 15: "Scientists with Half-closed Minds": Stevenson, 1958.

p. 16: His final paper: Stevenson, 2006.

CHAPTER 2

p. 27: Ian and Satwant published a paper: Stevenson & Pasricha, 1980.

p. 27: Ian also wrote it up: Stevenson, 1984.

p. 28: Samuel Johnson's line: Bartlett, 1968, p. 430.

p. 28: a young woman named Sumitra: Stevenson, Pasricha, and McClean-Rice, 1989.

pp. 28–29: "from that of a simple village girl": ibid., p. 84.

p. 29: a follow-up investigation: Mills & Dhiman, 2011.

p. 30: "although we do not dogmatically assert": Stevenson, Pasricha, and McClean-Rice, 1989, p. 100.

p. 31: As William James said: James, 1896, p. 5.

p. 37: They fed her eggs: Foll, 1959, and Khaing, 1962.

p. 37: a boy in Sri Lanka named Sujith: Stevenson, 1977.

p. 38: Ian wrote that he had to overcome: Stevenson, 2000a, p. 209.

p. 41: ones whose specifics: For a good example, see Sabom, 1998, chapter 3.

CHAPTER 3

p. 51: The airport claims: http://isleofbarra.com/for-visitors/the-airport/plane-landing-on-the-beach.html. Accessed 8/16/11.

p. 54: I developed a scale: Tucker, 2000.

p. 56: Child Dissociative Checklist: Putnam, Helmers, & Trickett, 1993.

p. 57: When our colleague Erlendur Haraldsson: Haraldsson, 1995 and 2003, and Haraldsson, Fowler, & Periyannanpillai, 2000.

p. 58: Swarnlata Mishra: Stevenson, 1974, pp. 67–91.

p. 61: when children report memories of two lives: Stevenson, 2000a, p. 218.

p. 61: in four of Ian's cases: ibid.

p. 61: F. W. H. Myers's: For a remarkable review of Myers, see Kelly, et al., 2007, chapter 2.

p. 62: a soul that originated in a spiritual environment: Myers, 1903, volume I, p. 34. I learned of Myers's model of the mind from a presentation by Adam Crabtree.

CHAPTER 4

p. 66: *Soul Survivor*: Leininger & Leininger, 2009.

p. 72: *The Battle for Iwo Jima 1945*: Wright, 1999.

p. 73: post-traumatic play: See American Academy of Child and Adolescent Psychiatry Staff, 2000; Wälder, 1933; and, most notably, Terr, 1981. For post-traumatic symptoms in children who report past-life memories, see Haraldsson, 2003.

p. 75: *Natoma Bay's* involvement in Iwo Jima: *Dictionary of American Naval Fighting Ships* (1970), pp. 22-23.

p. 75: eight pilots from *Natoma Bay* took part: This is taken from the *Natoma Bay* Iwo Jima Operations Report War Diary.

p. 79: 113 landings: Tillman, 1979.

CHAPTER 5

p. 103: families have often conducted: Stevenson, 2000a, pp. 113–115.

p. 103: Gnanatilleka: ibid. See also Tucker, 2005, pp. 151–156, and most definitively, Nissanka, 2001.

CHAPTER 6

p. 121: Ian and two colleagues wrote a paper: Stevenson, Pasricha, & Samararatne, 1988.

p. 125: Howard's death: White, 1977.

p. 132: "young Bobby": Reported at http://www.cnn.com /2011/US/04/07/bobby.jones.iv.grandfather.legacy/index .html. Retrieved on 8/12/12.

p. 134: a paper on abnormalities: Stevenson, 2000b.

p. 136: Ian speculated that women's lives: Stevenson, 1983, p. 223.

p. 137: five years of deaths in the United States: www.cdc .gov/nchs/data/misc/atlasres.pdf. Retrieved 9/24/12.

CHAPTER 7

p. 141: Erlendur Haraldsson, a colleague, has suggested: Haraldsson, 2003.

p. 146: "London Bridge Is Falling Down": *The Oxford Dictionary of Nursery Rhymes*, 1952, pp. 270–78.

p. 162: a tremendous need for timber: See McLaughlin, 1998, chapter 7.

p. 163: hooley: another source is http://en.wiktionary.org/wiki/hooley.

CHAPTER 8

p. 166: A recent study found that a quarter of scientists: Ecklund & Long, 2011.

p. 167: *The Language of God*: Collins, 2006.

p. 167: Brian Josephson: Klarreich, 2001.

p. 167: "We have known": http://wwwphysics.lbl.gov/~stapp/UCSF050509.docA, p. 3.

p. 168: "I regard consciousness as fundamental": *The Observer* (January 25, 1931). Cited in Stromberg, 1942, p. 329.

p. 169: called the double-slit experiment: For discussions of the double-slit experiment, see Greene, 1999; Davies, 1983; and The Double-Slit Experiment, 2002.

p. 169: An analogy would be the waves: Greene, 1999, p. 99.

p. 170: As Paul Dirac said: Dirac, 1958, p. 9.

p. 170: The double-slit experiment has now been done with electrons: See The Double-Slit Experiment, 2002, for details of the history of the experiments.

p. 170: neutrons, atoms, and even larger molecules: ibid.

p. 170: "impossible, *absolutely* impossible, to explain in any classical way": Feynman, Leighton, & Sands, 1963, volume 3, p. 1-1.

p. 170: "has in it the heart of quantum mechanics": ibid.

p. 171: "the atoms or the elementary particles themselves": Herbert, 1985, p. 195.

p. 171: "the transition from the 'possible'": Stapp, 2007, p. 90.

p. 172: Heisenberg called the potential outcomes *potentia*: Herbert, 1985, p. 195.

p. 172: John von Neumann, a brilliant mathematician who wrote a book: von Neumann, 1955 (original published in 1932).

p. 172: "quantum bible": Herbert, 1985, p. 25.

p. 172: Von Neumann discusses: For discussions of von Neumann's work, see Rosenblum & Kuttner, 2006, p. 184, and Herbert, 1985, pp. 145–149.

p. 173: "his abstract 'ego'": von Neumann, 1955, p. 421.

p. 173: "the intellectual inner life of the individual": ibid., p. 418.

p. 173: a physical signal in the brain: Herbert, 1985, p. 148.

p. 173: He produced a thought experiment: ibid., p. 160.

p. 174: "The wave function is collapsed": Henry, 2005.

p. 174: random event generators: Radin & Nelson, 1989.

p. 174: A researcher named Helmut Schmidt: Schmidt, 1993.

p. 175: French physicist Olivier Costa de Beauregard: Costa de Beauregard, 1995, p. 290.

p. 175: Few physicists would still give classical physics: Vedral, 2011.

p. 176: "shows that the universe is founded": Greene, 1999, p. 108.

p. 176: Schrödinger's famous cat: Gilder, 2008, p. 173, and Schrödinger, 1935.

p. 176: SQUID: Friedman, et al., 2000.

p. 177: "Schrödinger's SQUID": Collins, 2000.

p. 177: "Schrödinger's cat is now fat": Blatter, 2000.

p. 177: "New life for Schrödinger's cat": Leggett, 2000.

p. 177: physicists at University of California, Santa Barbara: O'Connell, et al., 2010.

p. 177: *Science* named it the Breakthrough of the Year: Cho, 2010.

p. 177: "A transition from quantum to classical": Seife, 2001.

p. 177: Numerous experiments, from Zeilinger and others: For example, see Arndt, et al., 1999; Nairz, et al., 2002; Friedman, et al., 2000; van der Wal, et al., 2000; Hackermüller, et al., 2003. Further examples are shown in Vedral, 2011, p. 42.

pp. 177–78: John Wheeler . . . imagined a thought experiment: Folger, 2002.

p. 178: This kind of delayed-choice experiment: See Jacques, et al., 2007, which also references previous studies.

p. 178: a similar thought experiment on a galactic scale: Folger, 2002.

p. 180: Albert Einstein was unhappy with quantum theory: Fine, 2011.

p. 180: not clear he even read the final draft: ibid.

p. 180: cited in physics journals far more than any other paper Einstein ever wrote: Gilder, 2008, pp. 3–4.

p. 180: EPR: Einstein, Podolsky, & Rosen, 1935. Quotes from p. 780.

p. 181: John Bell published a discussion: Bell, 1964.

p. 181: Bell's theorem: For a discussion, see Rosenblum & Kuttner, 2006, pp. 142–152.

p. 181: "Grossly non-local": Bell, 1964, p. 195.

p. 181: most notably by Alain Aspect: Aspect, Grangier, & Roger, 1981; Aspect, Dalibard, & Roger, 1982; Aspect, Grangier, & Roger, 1982.

p. 181: Bell wrote that requiring locality: Bell, 1964, p. 195.

p. 182: "Our world therefore does *not*": Rosenblum & Kuttner, 2006, p. 143.

p. 182: a group of physicists in Vienna published a study: Gröblacher, et al., 2007.

p. 182: "Quantum physics says goodbye to reality": http://physicsworld.com/cws/article/news/2007/apr/20/quantum-physics-says-goodbye-to-reality.

p. 182: "highly counterintuitive": ibid., p. 875.

p. 182: first proposed by Costa de Beauregard: See Jammer, 1974, pp. 238–239, and Costa de Beauregard, 1987, particularly p. 252.

p. 185: Stephen King dispensed: King, 2011, p. 61.

p. 185: "It is wrong to think of [the] past": Wheeler, 1983, p. 194.

p. 185: He wrote that since equipment operating in the present: ibid., pp. 194–196.

p. 185: "in some strange sense this is a 'participatory universe'": Wheeler, 1977, p. 6.

p. 185: "there is a sense in which what the observer will do": ibid., p. 3.

p. 186: "'observership' is a prerequisite": ibid.

p. 186: "acts of observer-participancy" could give "tangible 'reality'": Wheeler, 1983, p. 209.

p. 186: "You may ask whether the universe": Folger, 2002, p. 48.

p. 186: If some of the physical constants or initial conditions of the universe had been different: Wheeler, 1977.

p. 186: the odds of a low-entropy universe with formed matter: See Davies, 1983, chapters 12 and 13.

p. 187: the existence of God: See Collins, 2006.

p. 187: strong anthropic principle: Carter, 1974, and Barrow & Tippler, 1988.

p. 187: "Unless the blind dice of mutation": Wheeler, 1977, p. 28.

pp. 187–88: "It is well known that carbon": Dicke, 1961.

p. 188: thermonuclear combustion is required: Wheeler, 1977.

p. 188: " 'consciousness' has nothing whatsoever to do": Wheeler, 1983, p. 196.

p. 188: Though he only hinted at a consciousness-created reality: Herbert, 1985, p. 25.

p. 188: Wigner's friend: Wigner, 1962.

p. 189: "the being with a consciousness must have": ibid., p. 294.

p. 189: "it is the entering of an impression into our consciousness . . . unavoidably and unalterably": ibid., p. 289.

p. 189: He has written books: Stapp, 1996, 2007.

p. 189: "I do not know any sense": Folger, 2002, p. 48.

p. 189: "The universe begins to look more like a great thought": Jeans, 1933, p. 186.

pp. 189–90: "The doctrine that the world": d'Espagnat, 1979, p. 158.

p. 190: Everett's many-worlds interpretation: Everett, 1957. See also Herbert, 1985, for a discussion.

p. 190: Wheeler's stated reason: Wheeler, 1983.

pp. 190–91: "Brain function"—the mind—"will someday be explained": ibid., p. 207.

p. 191: "the observer is as essential": Wheeler, 1977, p. 27.

p. 191: Consciousness does not exist because the physical world does: This is similar to a statement by astronomer Bernard Haisch (2006): "It is not matter that creates an illusion of consciousness, but consciousness that creates an illusion of matter." I would not go so far as to say, however, that matter is purely an illusion, only that it only comes into existence out of consciousness.

p. 193: lucid dreams: See LaBerge, 1985.

p. 193: Gertrude Schmeidler: Schmeidler, 1943, and www
.parapsych.org/members/g_schmeidler.html.

p. 193: This finding has since been confirmed: Palmer, 1977.

CHAPTER 9

p. 195: Near-death experience (or NDEs). Much of this review of NDEs comes from Poonam Sharma: Sharma & Tucker, 2004.

p. 196: Allan Kellehear reviewed: Kellehear, 1993.

p. 196: Satwant Pasricha likewise found: Pasricha, 1995.

p. 197: Todd Murphy collected: Murphy, 2001.

p. 197: Yamatoots (the messengers . . .): Pasricha & Stevenson, 1986.

p. 197: Author Sam Harris recently made this argument: http://www.samharris.org/blog/item/science-on-the-brink -of-death.

p. 197: *Proof of Heaven*: Alexander, 2012.

p. 197: *Heaven Is for Real*: Burpo with Vincent, 2010.

p. 198: Poonam Sharma, a medical student: Sharma & Tucker, 2004.

p. 202: Burmese children who have talked about being Japanese soldiers: Stevenson & Keil, 2005.

p. 203: Only one systematic survey: Barker & Pasricha, 1979.

p. 204: Tibetan Buddhists: See Rinpoche, 1993, chapter 14.

p. 205: Mediumship, the idea: For an overview, see Gauld, 1982.

p. 207: deceased relatives on the other side: Kelly, 2001.

p. 207: deceased relatives they hadn't known were dead before they had their NDEs: Greyson, 2010.

p. 210: hypnotic regression proponents suggest: For ideas along these lines, see Weiss, 1988, and Newton, 1994.

p. 210: This seems similar to how species: The analogy to natural selection developed during a stimulating conversation I had with filmmaker David Sauvage.

p. 212: concept of synchronicity: Jung, 1952/1970.

p. 212: three types of synchronistic events: ibid., p. 526.

p. 212: Bernard Beitman: Beitman, 2011.

p. 213: another factor in nature: Jung, 1952/1970, p. 485.

p. 213: a man who was intensely studying: Main, 2007, p. 12.

p. 216: a single nerve cell in one large nervous system: Sir James Jeans made the same analogy: *The Observer* (4 January 1931).

p. 217: islands as William James suggested: James 1909/1986, p. 374.

References

Alexander, E. 2012. *Proof of Heaven: A Neurosurgeon's Journey into the Afterlife*. New York: Simon & Schuster.

American Academy of Child and Adolescent Psychiatry Staff. 2000. *Your Child: Emotional, Behavioral, and Cognitive Development from Birth Through Preadolescence*. Edited by D. Pruitt. New York: HarperCollins.

Arndt, M., O. Nairz, J. Vos-Andreae, C. Keller, G. van der Zouw, and A. Zellinger. 1999. "Wave-Particle Duality of C_{60} Molecules," *Nature* 401:680–682.

Aspect, A., J. Dalibard, and G. Roger. 1982. "Experimental Test of Bell's Inequalities Using Time-Varying Analyzers," *Physical Review Letters* 49:1804–1807.

Aspect, A., P. Grangier, and G. Roger. 1981. "Experimental Tests of Realistic Local Theories via Bell's Theorem." *Physical Review Letters* 47:460–463.

Aspect, A., P. Grangier, and G. Roger. 1982. "Experimental Realization of Einstein-Podolsky-Rosen-Bohm *Gedankenexperiment*: A New Violation of Bell's Inequalities," *Physical Review Letters* 49:91–94.

Barker, D. R., and S. K. Pasricha. 1979. "Reincarnation Cases in

Fatehabad: A Systematic Survey in North India," *Journal of Asian and African Studies* 14:231–240.

Barrow, J. D., and F. J. Tipler. 1988. *The Anthropic Cosmological Principle*. Oxford: Oxford University Press.

Bartlett, J. 1968. *Familiar quotations*. Edited by E. M. Beck. 14th edition. Boston: Little, Brown and Company. Original edition, 1855.

Beitman, B. D. 2011. "Coincidence Studies," *Psychiatric Annals* 41:561–571.

Bell, J. S. 1964. "On the Einstein Podolsky Rosen Paradox," *Physics* 1:195–200.

Blatter, G. 2000. "Schrödinger's Cat Is Now Fat," *Nature* 406: 25–26.

Bowman, C. 1997. *Children's Past Lives: How Past Life Memories Affect Your Child*. New York: Bantam Books.

Bowman, C. 2001. *Return from Heaven: Beloved Relatives Reincarnated Within Your Family*. New York: HarperCollins.

Burpo, T., with L. Vincent. 2010. *Heaven Is for Real: A Little Boy's Astounding Story of His Trip to Heaven and Back*. Nashville, Tennessee: Thomas Nelson.

Carter, B. 1974. "Large Number Coincidences and the Anthropic Principle in Cosmology," *Confrontations of Cosmological Theories with Observational Data*, edited by M. S. Longair. Dordrecht, Netherlands: D. Reidel.

Cho, A. 2010. "The First Quantum Machine," *Science* 330:1604.

Collins, F. S. 2006. *The Language of God: A Scientist Presents Evidence for Belief*. New York: Free Press.

Collins, G. P. 2000. "Schrödinger's SQUID," *Scientific American*, October.

Costa de Beauregard, O. 1987. "Time, the Physical Magnitude," edited by R. S. Cohen and M. W. Wartofsky. Vol. 99, *Boston*

Studies in the Philosophy of Science. Dordrecht, Netherlands: D. Reidel.

Costa de Beauregard, O. 1995. "Macroscopic Retrocausation," *Foundations of Physics Letters* 8 (3):287–291.

Davies, P. 1983. *God and the New Physics.* New York: Touchstone.

D'Espagnat, B. 1979. "The Quantum Theory and Reality," *Scientific American* 241 (5):158–181.

Dicke, R. H. 1961. "Dirac's Cosmology and Mach's Principle," *Nature* 192:440–441.

Dictionary of American Naval Fighting Ships, vol. 5. 1970. Washington: Defense Department, Navy, Naval History Division.

Dirac, P. A. M. 1958. *The Principles of Quantum Mechanics.* 4th ed. London: Oxford University Press.

The Double-Slit Experiment. 2002. *Physics World.* September, 15.

Ecklund, E. H., and E. Long. 2011. "Scientists and Spirituality," *Sociology of Religion.* 72:253–274.

Einstein, A., B. Podolsky, and N. Rosen. 1935. "Can Quantum-Mechanical Description of Physical Reality Be Considered Complete?" *Physical Review* 47:777–780.

Everett, H. 1957. "'Relative State' Formulation of Quantum Mechanics," *Reviews of Modern Physics* 29:454–462.

Feynman, R. P., R. B. Leighton, and M. Sands. 1963. *The Feynman Lectures on Physics.* 3 vols. Reading, Massachusetts: Addison-Wesley Publishing.

Fine, A. 2011. "The Einstein-Podolsky-Rosen Argument in Quantum Theory," *The Stanford Encyclopedia of Philosophy* (winter 2011 edition), edited by E. N. Zalta. http://plato.stanford.edu/archives/win2011/entries/qt-epr/.

Folger, T. 2002. "Does the Universe Exist if We're Not Looking?" *Discover,* June, 44–48.

Foll, C. V. 1959. "An Account of Some of the Beliefs and Superstitions About Pregnancy, Parturition and Infant Health in Burma," *Journal of Tropical Pediatrics* 5:51–59.

Friedman, J. R., V. Patel, W. Chen, S. K. Tolpygo, and J. E. Lukens. 2000. "Quantum Superposition of Distinct Macroscopic States," *Nature* 406:43–46.

Gauld, A. 1982. *Mediumship and Survival: A Century of Investigations.* London: William Heinemann.

Gilder, L. 2008. *The Age of Entanglement: When Quantum Physics Was Reborn.* New York: Alfred A. Knopf.

Greene, B. 1999. *The Elegant Universe: Superstrings, Hidden Dimensions, and the Quest for the Ultimate Theory.* New York: W. W. Norton.

Greyson, B. 2010. "Seeing Deceased Persons Not Known to Have Died: 'Peak in Darien' Experiences," *Anthropology and Humanism* 35:159–171.

Gröblacher, S., T. Paterek, R. Kaltenbaek, C. Brukner, M. Żukowski, M. Aspelmeyer, and A. Zeilinger. 2007. "An Experimental Test of Non-Local Realism," *Nature* 446:871–875.

Hackermüller, L., S. Uttenthaler, K. Hornberger, E. Reiger, Brezger B., A. Zeilinger, and M. Arndt. 2003. "Wave Nature of Biomolecules and Fluorofullerenes," *Physical Review Letters* 91:090408-1–090408-4.

Haisch, B. 2006. *The God Theory: Universes, Zero-Point Fields and What's Behind It All.* San Francisco: Weiser Books.

Haraldsson, E. 1995. "Personality and Abilities of Children Claiming Previous-Life Memories," *Journal of Nervous and Mental Disease* 183:445–451.

Haraldsson, E. 2003. "Children Who Speak of Past-Life Experiences: Is There a Psychological Explanation?" *Psychology and Psychotherapy: Theory, Research and Practice* 76:55–67.

Haraldsson, E., P. C. Fowler, and V. Periyannanpillai. 2000. "Psychological Characteristics of Children Who Speak of a Previous Life: A Further Field Study in Sri Lanka," *Transcultural Psychiatry* 37:525–544.

Henry, R. C. 2005. "The Mental Universe," *Nature* 436:29.

Herbert, N. 1985. *Quantum Reality: Beyond the New Physics*. New York: Anchor Books.

Jacques, V., E. Wu, F. Grosshans, F. Treussart, P. Grangier, A. Aspect, and J. Roch. 2007. "Experimental Realization of Wheeler's Delayed-Choice Gedanken Experiment," *Science* 315:966–968.

James, W. 1896. Presidential Address, *Proceedings of the Society for Psychical Research* 12:2–10.

James, W. 1909/1986. "Confidences of a 'Psychical Researcher,'" *Essays in Psychical Research*. Cambridge, Massachusetts: Harvard University Press.

Jammer, M. 1974. *The Philosophy of Quantum Mechanics: The Interpretations of Quantum Mechanics in Historical Perspective*. New York: John Wiley & Sons.

Jeans, J. 1933. *The Mysterious Universe*. Revised ed. New York: Macmillan.

Jung, C. G. 1952/1970. "Synchronicity: An Acausal Connecting Principle," trans., R.F.C. Hull, *The Structure and Dynamics of the Psyche*, edited by G. Adler, M. Fordham, and H. Read. Princeton, New Jersey: Princeton University Press.

Kellehear, A. 1993. "Culture, Biology, and the Near Death Experience: A Reappraisal." *Journal of Nervous and Mental Disease* 181:148–156.

Kelly, E. F., E. W. Kelly, A. Crabtree, A. Gauld, M. Grosso, and B. Greyson. 2007. *Irreducible Mind: Toward a Psychology for the 21st Century*. Lanham, Maryland: Rowman & Littlefield.

Kelly, E. W. 2001. "Near-Death Experiences with Reports of Meeting Deceased People," *Death Studies* 25:229–249.

Khaing, M. M. 1962. *Burmese Family*. Bloomington: Indiana University Press.

King, L. S. 1975. "Reincarnation," *JAMA* 234:978.

King, S. 2011. *11/22/63*. New York: Scribner.

Klarreich, E. 2001. "Stamp Booklet Has Physicists Licked," *Nature* 413:339.

LaBerge, S. 1985. *Lucid Dreaming*. Los Angeles: Jeremy P. Tarcher.

Leggett, T. 2000. "New Life for Schrödinger's Cat," *Physics World*, August, 23–24.

Leininger, B. and A. Leininger, with K. Gross. 2009. *Soul Survivor: The Reincarnation of a World War II Fighter Pilot*. New York: Grand Central.

Main, R. 2007. *Revelations of Chance*. Albany: State University of New York Press.

McLaughlin, M. 1998. *Sierra Stories: True Tales of Tahoe*. Carnelian Bay, California: Mic Mac.

Mills, A., and K. Dhiman. 2011. "Shiva Returned in the Body of Sumitra: A Posthumous Longitudinal Study of the Significance of the Shiva/Sumitra Case of the Possession Type," *Proceedings of the Society for Psychical Research* 59:145–193.

Moody, R. L. 1946. "Bodily Changes During Abreaction," *Lancet* 2:934–935.

Murphy, T. 2001. "Near-Death Experiences in Thailand," *Journal of Near-Death Studies* 19:161–178.

Myers, F. W. H. 1903. *Human Personality: And Its Survival of Bodily Death*. 2 vols. London: Longman's, Green.

Nairz, O., M. Arndt, and A. Zeilinger. 2002. "Experimental Verification of the Heisenberg Uncertainty Pprinciple for Fullerene Molecules," *Physical Review A* 65:032109-1–032109-4.

Newton, M. 1994. *Journey of Souls: Case Studies of Life Between Lives*. St. Paul, Minnesota: Llewellyn.

Nissanka, H. S. S. 2001. *The Girl Who Was Reborn: A Case-Study Suggestive of Reincarnation*. Colombo, Sri Lanka: Godage Brothers.

O'Connell, A. D., M. Hofheinz, M. Ansmann, R. C. Bialczak, M. Lenander, E. Lucero, M. Neeley, D. Sank, H. Wang, M. Weides, M. Wenner, J. M. Martinis, and A. N. Cleland. 2010. "Quantum Ground State and Single-Phonon Control of a Mechanical Resonator," *Nature* 464:697–703.

The Oxford Dictionary of Nursery Rhymes. 1952. Edited by I. Opie and P. Opie. London: Oxford University Press.

Palmer, J. 1977. "Attitudes and Personality Traits in Experimental ESP Research," *Handbook of Parapsychology*, edited by B. B. Wolman. New York: Van Nostrand Reinhold.

Pasricha, S. 1995. "Near Death Experiences in South India: A Systematic Survey," *Journal of Scientific Exploration* 9:79–88.

Pasricha, S. K., J. Keil, J. B. Tucker, and I. Stevenson. 2005. "Some Bodily Malformations Attributed to Previous Lives," *Journal of Scientific Exploration* 19:359–383.

Pasricha, S., and I. Stevenson. 1986. "Near-Death Experiences in India: A Preliminary Report," *Journal of Nervous and Mental Disease* 174:165–170.

Putnam, F. W., K. Helmers, and P. K. Trickett. 1993. "Development, Reliability, and Validity of a Child Dissociation Scale," *Child Abuse & Neglect* 17:731–741.

Radin, D. I., and R. D. Nelson. 1989. "Evidence for Consciousness-Related Anomalies in Random Physical Systems," *Foundations of Physics* 19:1499–1514.

Rinpoche, S. 1993. *The Tibetan Book of Living and Dying*. New York: HarperCollins.

Rosenblum, B., and F. Kuttner. 2006. *Quantum Enigma: Physics*

Encounters Consciousness. New York: Oxford University Press.

Sabom, M. 1998. *Light & Death: One Doctor's Fascinating Account of Near-Death Experiences.* Grand Rapids, Michigan: Zondervan Publishing House.

Schmeidler, G. R. 1943. "Predicting Good and Bad Scores in a Clairvoyance Experiment: A Final Report," *Journal of the American Society for Psychical Research* 37:210–221.

Schmidt, H. 1993. "Observation of a Psychokinetic Effect Under Highly Controlled Conditions," *Journal of Parapsychology* 57:351–372.

Schrödinger, E. 1935. "Die Gegenwärtige Situation in der Quantenmechanik" [The present situation in quantum mechanics] *Die Naturwissenschaften* [*The Natural Sciences*] 48:807–812, 823–828, 844–849.

Seife, C. 2001. "Microscale Weirdness Expands Its Turf," *Science* 292 (5521):1471.

Shroder, T. 1999. *Old Souls: The Scientific Evidence for Past Lives.* New York: Simon & Schuster.

Shroder, T. 2008. "A Good Question," *Journal of Scientific Exploration* 22:115–116.

Stapp, H. P. 1996. *Mind, Matter and Quantum Mechanics.* Berlin: Springer.

Stapp, H. P. 2007. *Mindful Universe: Quantum Mechanics and the Participating Observer.* Berlin: Springer.

Stevenson, I. 1958. "Scientists with Half-Closed Minds." *Harper's Magazine* 217:64–71.

Stevenson, I. 1974. *Twenty Cases Suggestive of Reincarnation.* 2nd rev. ed. Charlottesville: University Press of Virginia. (First published in 1966 in *Proceedings of the American Society for Psychical Research*, vol. 26.)

Stevenson, I. 1977. *Cases of the Reincarnation Type, vol. II: Ten*

Cases in Sri Lanka. Charlottesville: University Press of Virginia.

Stevenson, I. 1978. "Some Comments on Automatic Writing," *Journal of the American Society for Psychical Research* 72:315–332.

Stevenson, I. 1983. *Cases of the Reincarnation Type, vol. IV: Twelve Cases in Thailand and Burma*. Charlottesville: University Press of Virginia.

Stevenson, I. 1984. *Unlearned Language: New Studies in Xenoglossy*. Charlottesville: University Press of Virginia.

Stevenson, I. 1993. "Birthmarks and Birth Defects Corresponding to Wounds on Deceased Persons," *Journal of Scientific Exploration* 7:403–416.

Stevenson, I. 1997. *Reincarnation and Biology: A Contribution to the Etiology of Birthmarks and Birth Defects*. Westport, Connecticut: Praeger.

Stevenson, I. 1999. "Past Lives of Twins," *Lancet* 353:1359–1360.

Stevenson, I. 2001. *Children Who Remember Previous Lives: A Question of Reincarnation*. Revised ed. Jefferson, North Carolina: McFarland.

Stevenson, I. 2000. "The Phenomenon of Claimed Memories of Previous Lives: Possible Interpretations and Importance," *Medical Hypotheses* 54 (4):652–659.

Stevenson, I. 2006. "Half a Career with the Paranormal," *Journal of Scientific Exploration* 20:13–21.

Stevenson, I., and J. Keil. 2005. "Children of Myanmar Who Behave Like Japanese Soldiers: A Possible Third Element in Personality." *Journal of Scientific Exploration* 19:171–183.

Stevenson, I., and S. Pasricha. 1980. "A Preliminary Report on an Unusual Case of the Reincarnation Type with Xenoglossy," *Journal of the American Society for Psychical Research* 74:331–348.

Stevenson, I., S. Pasricha, and N. McClean-Rice. 1989. "A Case of the Possession Type in India with Evidence of Paranormal Knowledge," *Journal of Scientific Exploration* 3:81–101.

Stevenson, I., S. Pasricha, and G. Samararatne. 1988. "Deception and Self-Deception in Cases of the Reincarnation Type: Seven Illustrative Cases in Asia," *Journal of the American Society for Psychical Research* 82:1–31.

Stromberg, G. 1942. "Coherence in a Physical World," *Philosophy of Science* 9:323–334.

Terr, L. C. 1981. "Forbidden Games: Post-traumatic child's play," *Journal of the American Academy of Child Psychiatry* 20:741–760.

Tillman, B. 1979. *Corsair: The F4U in World War II and Korea*. Annapolis, Maryland: Naval Institute Press.

Tucker, J. B. 2000. "A Scale to Measure the Strength of Children's Claims of Previous Lives: Methodology and Initial Findings," *Journal of Scientific Exploration* 14:571–581.

Tucker, J. B. 2005. *Life Before Life: A Scientific Investigation of Children's Memories of Previous Lives*. New York: St. Martin's Press.

van der Wal, C. H., A. C. J. ter Haar, F. K. Wilhelm, R. N. Schouten, C. J. P. M. Harmans, T. P. Orlando, S. Lloyd, and J. E. Mooij. 2000. "Quantum Superposition of Macroscopic Persistent-Current States." *Science* 290:773–777.

Vedral, V. 2011. "Living in a Quantum World," *Scientific American*, June, 38–43.

von Neumann, J. 1955. *Mathematical Foundations of Quantum Mechanics*. Translated by R. T. Beyer. Princeton, New Jersey: Princeton University Press.

Wälder, R. 1933. "The Psychoanalytic Theory of Play," *Psychoanalytic Quarterly* 2:208–224.

Weiss, B. 1988. *Many Lives, Many Masters: The True Story of a*

Prominent Psychiatrist, His Young Patient, and the Past-Life Therapy That Changed Both Their Lives. New York: Fireside.

Wheeler, J. A. 1977. "Genesis and Observership," *Foundational Problems in the Special Sciences*, edited by R. Butts and J. Hintikka. Dordrecht, Netherlands: D. Reidel.

Wheeler, J. A. 1983. "Law Without Law," *Quantum Theory and Measurement*, edited by J. Wheeler and W. H. Zurek. Princeton, New Jersey: Princeton University Press.

White, S. H. 1977. *Sidney Howard*. Boston: Twayne.

Wigner, E. P. 1962. "Remarks on the Mind-Body Question," *The Scientist Speculates: An Anthropology of Partly-Baked Ideas*, edited by I. J. Good. New York: Basic Books.

Wright, D. 1999. *The Battle for Two Jima 1945*. Stroud, England: Sutton.

